Language Arts 800
Teacher's Guide

CONTENTS

Author: **Alpha Omega Publications**

Editor: Alan Christopherson, M.S.

Alpha Omega Publications®

804 N. 2nd Ave. E., Rock Rapids, IA 51246-1759

OVERVIEW

LANGUAGE ARTS

Curriculum Overview
Grades K–12

◼━━━━━━━━━━━━◼

Kindergarten

Language Arts Lessons

1-40	41-80	81-120	121-160
Alphabet-say the alphabet **Colors-**recognize colors **Directions-**left to right **Following directions-**given once **Grammar-**form simple sentences **Listening skills** **Personal recognition-**read and write first name -know age and address -recognize names of family members **Phonics-**short *a, e, i* vowels -initial: *b, t, m, r, s, n, d, p, l* -form and read simple words -form rhyming words **Shapes-**circle, square, triangle, and rectangle -recognize shapes in objects **Stories and Poems-**create simple stories and poems **Writing-**form circle and lines -*Aa, Bb, Dd, Ee, Ii, Ll, Mm, Nn, Pp, Rr, Ss,* and *Tt*	**Grammar-**sentences begin with capital, end with period **Patterns-**simple shape, color patterns **Personal recognition-**read and write first and last name **Phonics-**short *a, e, i, o, and u* vowels -initial: *k, c, ck, f, h, g, j, v, w, y, z, qu, and x* -read simple sentences **Position/direction concepts-**in/out, in front of/behind, up/down, on/off, open/closed, over/under **Sequencing-**alphabetical order -simple story **Shapes-**oval **Size concepts-**big/little, large/small **Writing-***Kk, Cc, Ff, Hh, Oo, Gg, Jj, Vv, Ww, Uu, Yy, Zz, Qq,* and *Xx*	**Phonics-**recognize the short vowel sounds -recognize all initial consonant sounds -recognize long *a, e, i, o,* and *u* sounds -silent *e* -initial consonant digraphs: *sh, ch,* both soft and hard *th* -final consonant sounds: _*b,* _*ck,* _*k,* _*l* **Word recognition-**color words, number words & shape words **Writing-**name -complete alphabet, capital and small letters -all color words -number words: *one, two, three, four, five, six* -shape words: *circle, square, triangle*	**Phonics-**recognize the long vowel sounds -initial consonant diagraphs: *wh;* review *ch, sh, th* -recognize all final consonant sounds: **Stories and poems-**create, tell, and recite stories and poems **Word recognition-**position/direction words: *up/down, high/low, in, inside, out, outside, top/bottom* -number words: *seven, eight, nine, ten* -shape words: *rectangle, oval, star* **Writing-**number words: *seven, eight, nine, ten* -shape words: *rectangle, oval, star* -position/direction words: *up/down, high/low, in, inside, out, outside, top/bottom*

Language Arts LIFEPAC Overview

	Grade 1	Grade 2	Grade 3
LIFEPAC 1	**FUN WITH PHONICS** • Short vowel sounds • Consonants • Main ideas • Rhyming words	**KNOW YOUR NOUNS** • Review vowels & consonants • Beginning, middle, ending sounds • Singular & plural nouns • Common & proper nouns	**OLD AND NEW SKILLS** • Vowels • Consonants • Sentence phrases • Capital letters • Reading skills
LIFEPAC 2	**FUN WITH PHONICS** • Kinds of sentences • Cardinal & ordinal numbers • Suffixes • Plurals • Classifying	**ACTION VERBS** • Vowel digraphs • Action words – verbs • Following directions • The dictionary • ABC order	**BUILDING WORDS • SENTENCES** • Vowels – long, short • Questions • ABC order • Capital letters
LIFEPAC 3	**FUN WITH PHONICS** • Consonant digraphs • Compounds • Syllables • Possessives • Contractions • Soft c and g	**SIMPLE SENTENCES** • r-controlled vowels • Consonant blends • Using capital letters • Subjects & verbs in sentences	**WORDS • GETTING TO THE ROOTS** • Root words • Dictionary guide words • Synonyms • Antonyms • Capital letters
LIFEPAC 4	**FUN WITH PHONICS** • Paragraphs • Silent letters • Sequencing • Subject-verb agreement	**TYPES OF SENTENCES** • Consonant digraphs • Statement, question, exclamation sentences • Using capital letters • The library	**WORDS • HOW TO USE THEM** • Noun • Verb • Adjective • Adverb • Irregular vowels • Composition
LIFEPAC 5	**FUN WITH PHONICS** • Long vowels • Homonyms • Poetry • Syllables • Possessives • Contractions • Plurals • Suffixes	**USING PUNCTUATION** • Diphthongs • Punctuation review • Using a comma • Rules for making words plural • Writing a biography • Contractions	**SENTENCE • START TO FINISH** • Main idea • Capital letters and punctuation • Paragraphs • Making words plural
LIFEPAC 6	**FUN WITH PHONICS** • R-controlled vowels • Writing stories • Pronouns • Following directions	**ADJECTIVES** • Rhyming words • Biblical poetry • Adjectives in sentences • Synonyms, antonyms • Thesaurus • Comparative, superlative adjectives	**ALL ABOUT BOOKS** • Main idea • Books • Stories • Poems • Critical thinking
LIFEPAC 7	**FUN WITH PHONICS** • Vowel digraphs • Letters - business, friendly, invitations • Syllables	**POSSESSIVE NOUNS** • Introduction to letter writing • Pronunciation key • Possessive nouns • Silent consonants • Homonyms	**READING AND WRITING** • For directions • Friendly letters • Pronouns • Fact • Fiction
LIFEPAC 8	**FUN WITH PHONICS** • Vowel digraphs • Subject-verb agreement • Compounds • Contractions • Possessives • Pronouns	**PRONOUNS** • Author's intent & use of titles • Predicting content • Suffixes • Character, setting, & plot • Analogies • Writing in cursive	**READING SKILLS** • For sequence • For detail • Verbs - being, compound • Drama
LIFEPAC 9	**FUN WITH PHONICS** • Vowel digraphs • Titles • Main ideas • Sentences • Paragraphs • Proper nouns	**VERB TYPES AND TENSES** • Review action verbs • Dividing words into syllables • State of being verbs • Past & present verb tenses	**MORE READING & WRITING** • For information • Thank you letters • Book reports • Reference books
LIFEPAC 10	**LOOKING BACK** • Letters and sounds • Contractions • Plurals • Possessives • Sentences • Stories	**LOOKING BACK** • Nouns & verbs • Word division • Consonant blends, digraphs • Prefixes, suffixes, root words • Possessives • Pronouns, adjectives	**LOOKING BACK** • Reading for comprehension • Sentence punctuation • Writing letters • Parts of Speech

Grade 4	Grade 5	Grade 6	
WRITTEN COMMUNICATION • Word derivations • Story sequence • Writing an outline • Writing a report	**STORY MESSAGES** • Main idea • Plot • Character • Setting • Dialogue • Diphthong • Digraph	**READING FOR A PURPOSE** • Critical thinking • Research data • Parables • Synonyms	LIFEPAC 1
SOUNDS TO WORDS • Hard and soft – c and g • Parts of dictionary • Accented syllables • Haiku Poetry	**MAIN IDEAS** • Poetry • Story • Synonyms • Compounds • Topic sentence • Adjectives • Nouns	**FORMING NEW WORDS** • Prefixes • Suffixes • Synonyms • Antonyms • Adjectives • Adverbs • Critical thinking	LIFEPAC 2
WORDS • HOW TO USE THEM • Prefixes • Suffixes • Homonyms • Antonyms • Poetry • Stories • Writing an outline	**WORDS TO STORIES** • Subject • Predicate • Adverbs • Idioms • Critical thinking • Writing a short story	**BETTER READING** • Story elements • Author's purpose • Information sources • Outline	LIFEPAC 3
MORE WORDS • HOW TO USE THEM • Parts of speech • Possession • Written directions • Verb tenses	**WRITTEN REPORT** • Outline • Four types of sentences • Metaphor • Simile • Writing the report	**SENTENCES** • Capitals • Punctuation • Four types of sentences • Author's purpose • Propaganda	LIFEPAC 4
WRITING FOR CLARITY • Figures of speech • Capital letters • Punctuation marks • Writing stories	**STORY ELEMENTS** • Legend • Implied meaning • Dialogue • Quotations • Word order • Usage • Story elements	**READING SKILLS** • Following directions • Literary forms • Phrases • Nouns • Verbs • Paragraph structure	LIFEPAC 5
FUN WITH FICTION • Book reports • Fiction • Nonfiction • Parables • Fables • Poetry	**POETRY** • Rhythm • Stanza • Symbolism • Personification • Irregular plurals	**POETRY** • Similes • Metaphors • Alliteration • Homonyms • Palindromes • Acronyms • Figures of speech	LIFEPAC 6
FACT AND FICTION • Nouns • Verbs • Contractions • Biography • Fables • Tall Tales	**WORD USAGE** • Nouns - common, plural, possessive • Fact • Opinion • Story • Main idea	**STORIES** • Story elements • Nouns • Pronouns • Vowel digraphs • Business letter	LIFEPAC 7
GRAMMAR AND WRITING • Adjectives to compare • Adverbs • Figurative language • Paragraphs	**ALL ABOUT VERBS** • Tense • Action • Participles • Of being • Regular • Irregular • Singular • Plural	**NEWSPAPERS** • Propaganda • News stories • Verbs – auxiliary, tenses • Adverbs	LIFEPAC 8
THE WRITTEN REPORT • Planning a report • Finding information • Outline • Writing a report	**READING FLUENCY** • Speed reading • Graphic aids • Study skills • Literary forms	**READING THE BIBLE** • Parables • Proverbs • Hebrew - poetry, prophecy • Bible history • Old Testament law	LIFEPAC 9
LOOKING BACK • Reading skills • Nouns • Adverbs • Written communication • Literary forms	**LOOKING BACK** • Literary forms • Parts of speech • Writing skills • Study skills	**LOOKING BACK** • Literary forms • Writing letters • Parts of speech • Punctuation	LIFEPAC 10

Language Arts LIFEPAC Overview

	Grade 7	Grade 8	Grade 9
LIFEPAC 1	**WORD USAGE** • Nouns – proper, common • Pronouns • Prefixes • Suffixes • Synonyms • Antonyms	**IMPROVE COMMUNICATION** • Roots • Inflections • Affixes • Interjections • Directions – oral, written • Non-verbal communication	**STRUCTURE OF LANGUAGE** • Nouns • Adjectives • Verbs • Prepositions • Adverbs • Conjunctions • Sentence parts

LIFEPAC 2	**MORE WORD USAGE**
	• Speech – stress, pitch
	• Verbs – tenses
	• Principle parts
	• Story telling
		ALL ABOUT ENGLISH
		• Origin of language
		• Classification–
		  nouns, pronouns, verbs,
		  adjectives, adverbs
			NATURE OF LANGUAGE
			• Origin of language
			• Use – oral and written
			• Dictionary
			• Writing a paper

LIFEPAC 3	**BIOGRAPHIES** • Biography as a form • Flashback technique • Deductive reasoning • Words – base, root	**PUNCTUATION AND WRITING** • Connecting and interrupting • The Essay • Thesis Statement	**PRACTICAL ENGLISH** • Dictionary use • Mnemonics • Writing a paper • Five minute speech
LIFEPAC 4	**LANGUAGE STRUCTURE** • Verbs – tenses • Principle parts • Sentence creativity • Speech – pitch, accent	**WORDS • HOW TO USE THEM** • Dictionary • Thesaurus • Accent • Diacritical mark • Standard • Nonstandard	**SHORT STORY FUNDAMENTALS** • Plot • Setting • Characterization • Conflict • Symbolism
LIFEPAC 5	**NATURE OF ENGLISH** • Formal • Informal • Redundant expressions • Verb tenses • Subject–verb agreement	**CORRECT LANGUAGE** • Using good form • Synonyms • Antonyms • Homonyms • Good speaking qualities	**LANGUAGE IN LITERATURE** • Collective Nouns • Verbs • Use of comparisons • Gerunds • Participles • Literary genres

LIFEPAC 6	**MECHANICS OF ENGLISH**
	• Punctuation
	• Complements • Modifiers
	• Clauses – subordinate,
	  coordinate
		LANGUAGE AND LITERATURE
		• History of English
		• Coordination and
		  subordination
		• Autobiography
			MEANING IN PROSE AND POETRY
			• Author's purpose and meaning
			• Meaning of structure
			• Factors of persuasion
			• Understanding poetry

LIFEPAC 7	**THE NOVEL**
	• The Hiding Place
	• Sequence of events
	• Author's purpose
	• Character sketch
		CRITICAL THINKING
		• Word evaluation
		• The Paragraph –
		  structure, coherence,
		  introductory, concluding
			COMMUNICATION
			• Planning a speech
			• Listening comprehension
			• Letters – business,
			  informal, social

LIFEPAC 8	**LITERATURE** • Nonfiction • Listening skills • Commas • Semicolons • Nonverbal communications	**WRITE • LISTEN • READ** • Business letters • Personal letters • Four steps to listen • Nonfiction	**LIBRARY AND DRAMA** • Library resources • Drama – history, elements, reading • The Miracle Worker
LIFEPAC 9	**COMPOSITIONS** • Sentence types • Quality of paragraph • Pronunciation • Nonsense literature	**SPEAK AND WRITE** • Etymology • Modifiers • Person • Number • Tense • Oral report	**STUDIES IN THE NOVEL** • History • Define • Write • Critical essay • Twenty Thousand Leagues Under the Sea
LIFEPAC 10	**LOOKING BACK** • Parts of speech • Sentence structure • Punctuation • How to communicate	**LOOKING BACK** • Composition structure • Parts of speech • Critical thinking • Literary forms	**LOOKING BACK** • Communication – writing speaking, listening • Using resources • Literature review

Grade 10	Grade 11	Grade 12	
EVOLUTION OF ENGLISH • Historical development • Varieties of English • Substandard & standard • Changes in English	**STANDARD ENGLISH** • Need for standard English • Guardians of the standard • Dictionaries • Types of standard English texts	**THE WORTH OF WORDS** • Word categories • Expository writing • Sentence structure • Diction	LIFEPAC 1
LISTENING AND SPEAKING • Noun plurals • Suffixes • Creating a speech • Nature of listening	**EFFECTIVE SENTENCES** • Subordinate – clauses, conjunctions • Relative pronouns • Verbals • Appositives	**STRUCTURE OF LANGUAGE** • Parts of speech • Sentence structure • Subordinate phrases • Subordinate clauses	LIFEPAC 2
EFFECTIVE SENTENCES • Participles • Infinitives • Prepositions • Gerunds • Sentences – simple, compound, complex	**SENTENCE WORKSHOP** • Understanding pronouns • Using pronouns correctly • Using modifiers correctly • Parallel sentence structure	**READ, RESEARCH, LISTEN** • Reading skills • Resources for research • Taking notes • Drawing conclusions	LIFEPAC 3
POWER OF WORDS • Etymology • Connotations • Poetic devices • Poetry – literal, figurative, symbolic	**WHY STUDY READING?** • Greek and Latin roots • Diacritical markings • Finding the main idea • Analyzing a textbook	**GIFT OF LANGUAGE** • Origin–Biblical, • Koine Greek • Purpose of Grammar • Semantics	LIFEPAC 4
ELEMENTS OF COMPOSITION • Paragraphs • Connectives • Transitions • Expository writing – elements, ideas	**POETRY** • Metrical feet • Sets • Musical effects • Universality • Imagery • Connotation	**ENGLISH LITERATURE** • Early England • Medieval England • Fourteenth century • Chaucer	LIFEPAC 5

STRUCTURE AND READING
• Subordinate clauses
• Pronouns – gender,
    case, agreement
• Reading for recognition
	NONFICTION
	• Elements
	• Types – essays, diaries,
	    newspaper, biography
	• Composition
		ELIZABETHAN LITERATURE
		• Poetry
		• Prose
		• Drama
		• Essay
			LIFEPAC 6

ORAL READING AND DRAMA • Skills of oral reading • Drama – history, irony elements, allegory • Everyman	**AMERICAN DRAMA** • Development • History • Structure • Purpose • Our Town	**17TH—18TH CENTURY LITERATURE** • Historical background • Puritan literature • Common sense – satire • Sensibility	LIFEPAC 7
THE SHORT STORY • Elements • Enjoying • Writing • The Literary Critique	**AMERICAN NOVEL** • Eighteenth, nineteenth twentieth century • The Old Man and the Sea • The Critical Essay	**WRITING • SHORT STORY, POETRY** • Fundamentals • Inspiration • Technique and style • Form and process	LIFEPAC 8
THE NOVEL • Elements • In His Steps • The Critical Essay • The Book Review	**COMPOSITION** • Stating the thesis • Research • Outline • Writing the paper	**POETRY • ROMANTIC , VICTORIAN** • Wordsworth • Coleridge • Gordon • Byron • Shelley • Keats • Tennyson • Hopkins • Robert and Elizabeth B Browning	LIFEPAC 9

LOOKING BACK
• Writing skills
• Speech skills
• Poetry • Drama
• Short stories • Novel
	LOOKING BACK
	• Analyzing written word
	• Effective sentences
	• Expository prose
	• Genres of American literature
		LOOKING BACK
		• Creative writing
		• English literature –
		    Medieval to
		    Victorian
			LIFEPAC 10

MANAGEMENT

STRUCTURE OF THE LIFEPAC CURRICULUM

The LIFEPAC curriculum is conveniently structured to provide one teacher handbook containing teacher support material with answer keys and ten student worktexts for each subject at grade levels two through twelve. The worktext format of the LIFEPACs allows the student to read the textual information and complete workbook activities all in the same booklet. The easy to follow LIFEPAC numbering system lists the grade as the first number(s) and the last two digits as the number of the series. For example, the Language Arts LIFEPAC at the 6th grade level, 5th book in the series would be LAN0605.

Each LIFEPAC is divided into 3 to 5 sections and begins with an introduction or overview of the booklet as well as a series of specific learning objectives to give a purpose to the study of the LIFEPAC. The introduction and objectives are followed by a vocabulary section which may be found at the beginning of each section at the lower levels, at the beginning of the LIFEPAC in the middle grades, or in the glossary at the high school level. Vocabulary words are used to develop word recognition and should not be confused with the spelling words introduced later in the LIFEPAC. The student should learn all vocabulary words before working the LIFEPAC sections to improve comprehension, retention, and reading skills.

Each activity or written assignment has a number for easy identification, such as 1.1. The first number corresponds to the LIFEPAC section and the number to the right of the decimal is the number of the activity.

Teacher checkpoints, which are essential to maintain quality learning, are found at various locations throughout the LIFEPAC. The teacher should check 1) neatness of work and penmanship, 2) quality of understanding (tested with a short oral quiz), 3) thoroughness of answers (complete sentences and paragraphs, correct spelling, etc.), 4) completion of activities (no blank spaces), and 5) accuracy of answers as compared to the answer key (all answers correct).

The self test questions are also number coded for easy reference. For example, 2.015 means that this is the 15th question in the self test of Section II. The first number corresponds to the LIFEPAC section, the zero indicates that it is a self test question, and the number to the right of the zero the question number.

The LIFEPAC test is packaged at the centerfold of each LIFEPAC. It should be removed and put aside before giving the booklet to the student for study.

Answer and test keys have the same numbering system as the LIFEPACs and appear at the back of this handbook. The student may be given access to the answer keys (not the test keys) under teacher supervision so that he can score his own work.

A thorough study of the Curriculum Overview by the teacher before instruction begins is essential to the success of the student. The teacher should become familiar with expected skill mastery and understand how these grade level skills fit into the overall skill development of the curriculum. The teacher should also preview the objectives that appear at the beginning of each LIFEPAC for additional preparation and planning.

TEST SCORING and GRADING

Answer keys and test keys give examples of correct answers. They convey the idea, but the student may use many ways to express a correct answer. The teacher should check for the essence of the answer, not for the exact wording. Many questions are high level and require thinking and creativity on the part of the student. Each answer should be scored based on whether or not the main idea written by the student matches the model example. "Any Order" or "Either Order" in a key indicates that no particular order is necessary to be correct.

Most self tests and LIFEPAC tests at the lower elementary levels are scored at 1 point per answer; however, the upper levels may have a point system awarding 2 to 5 points for various answers or questions. Further, the total test points will vary; they may not always equal 100 points. They may be 78, 85, 100, 105, etc.

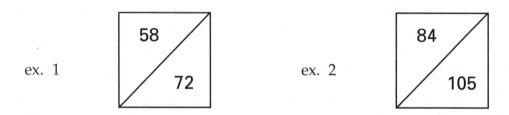

A score box similar to ex.1 above is located at the end of each self test and on the front of the LIFEPAC test. The bottom score, 72, represents the total number of points possible on the test. The upper score, 58, represents the number of points your student will need to receive an 80% or passing grade. If you wish to establish the exact percentage that your student has achieved, find the total points of his correct answers and divide it by the bottom number (in this case 72.) For example, if your student has a point total of 65, divide 65 by 72 for a grade of 90%. Referring to ex. 2, on a test with a total of 105 possible points, the student would have to receive a minimum of 84 correct points for an 80% or passing grade. If your student has received 93 points, simply divide the 93 by 105 for a percentage grade of 89%. Students who receive a score below 80% should review the LIFEPAC and retest using the appropriate Alternate Test found in the Teacher's Guide.

The following is a guideline to assign letter grades for completed LIFEPACs based on a maximum total score of 100 points.

LIFEPAC Test   =   60% of the Total Score (or percent grade)
Self Test   =   25% of the Total Score (average percent of self tests)
Reports   =   10% or 10* points per LIFEPAC
Oral Work   =   5% or 5* points per LIFEPAC
*Determined by the teacher's subjective evaluation of the student's daily work.

Example:

LIFEPAC Test Score	=	92%	92	x	.60		=	55 points
Self Test Average	=	90%	90	x	.25		=	23 points
Reports							=	8 points
Oral Work							=	4 points

TOTAL POINTS   =   90 points

Grade Scale based on point system:	100	–	94	=	A
	93	–	86	=	B
	85	–	77	=	C
	76	–	70	=	D
	Below		70	=	F

TEACHER HINTS and STUDYING TECHNIQUES

LIFEPAC Activities are written to check the level of understanding of the preceding text. The student may look back to the text as necessary to complete these activities; however, a student should never attempt to do the activities without reading (studying) the text first. Self tests and LIFEPAC tests are never open book tests.

Language arts activities (skill integration) often appear within other subject curriculum. The purpose is to give the student an opportunity to test his skill mastery outside of the context in which it was presented.

Writing complete answers (paragraphs) to some questions is an integral part of the LIFEPAC Curriculum in all subjects. This builds communication and organization skills, increases understanding and retention of ideas, and helps enforce good penmanship. Complete sentences should be encouraged for this type of activity. Obviously, single words or phrases do not meet the intent of the activity, since multiple lines are given for the response.

Review is essential to student success. Time invested in review where review is suggested will be time saved in correcting errors later. Self tests, unlike the section activities, are closed book. This procedure helps to identify weaknesses before they become too great to overcome. Certain objectives from self tests are cumulative and test previous sections; therefore, good preparation for a self test must include all material studied up to that testing point.

The following procedure checklist has been found to be successful in developing good study habits in the LIFEPAC curriculum.

1. Read the introduction and Table of Contents.
2. Read the objectives.
3. Recite and study the entire vocabulary (glossary) list.
4. Study each section as follows:
    a. Read the introduction and study the section objectives.
    b. Read all the text for the entire section, but answer none of the activities.
    c. Return to the beginning of the section and memorize each vocabulary word and definition.
    d. Reread the section, complete the activities, check the answers with the answer key, correct all errors, and have the teacher check.
    e. Read the self test but do not answer the questions.
    f. Go to the beginning of the first section and reread the text and answers to the activities up to the self test you have not yet done.
    g. Answer the questions to the self test without looking back.
    h. Have the self test checked by the teacher.
    i. Correct the self test and have the teacher check the corrections.
    j. Repeat steps a–i for each section.

5. Use the SQ3R* method to prepare for the LIFEPAC test.
6. Take the LIFEPAC test as a closed book test.
7. LIFEPAC tests are administered and scored under direct teacher supervision. Students who receive scores below 80% should review the LIFEPAC using the SQ3R* study method and take the Alternate Test located in the Teacher Handbook. The final test grade may be the grade on the Alternate Test or an average of the grades from the original LIFEPAC test and the Alternate Test.

  *SQ3R: **S**can the whole LIFEPAC.
  Question yourself on the objectives.
  Read the whole LIFEPAC again.
  Recite through an oral examination.
  Review weak areas.

GOAL SETTING and SCHEDULES

Each school must develop its own schedule, because no single set of procedures will fit every situation. The following is an example of a daily schedule that includes the five LIFEPAC subjects as well as time slotted for special activities.

Possible Daily Schedule

8:15	–	8:25	Pledges, prayer, songs, devotions, etc.
8:25	–	9:10	Bible
9:10	–	9:55	Language Arts
9:55	–	10:15	Recess (juice break)
10:15	–	11:00	Mathematics
11:00	–	11:45	Social Studies
11:45	–	12:30	Lunch, recess, quiet time
12:30	–	1:15	Science
1:15	–		Drill, remedial work, enrichment*

*Enrichment: Computer time, physical education, field trips, fun reading, games and puzzles, family business, hobbies, resource persons, guests, crafts, creative work, electives, music appreciation, projects.

Basically, two factors need to be considered when assigning work to a student in the LIFEPAC curriculum.

The first is time. An average of 45 minutes should be devoted to each subject, each day. Remember, this is only an average. Because of extenuating circumstances a student may spend only 15 minutes on a subject one day and the next day spend 90 minutes on the same subject.

The second factor is the number of pages to be worked in each subject. A single LIFEPAC is designed to take 3 to 4 weeks to complete. Allowing about 3-4 days for LIFEPAC introduction, review, and tests, the student has approximately 15 days to complete the LIFEPAC pages. Simply take the number of pages in the LIFEPAC, divide it by 15 and you will have the number of pages that must be completed on a daily basis to keep the student on schedule. For example, a LIFEPAC containing 45 pages will require 3 completed pages per day. Again, this is only an average. While working a 45 page LIFEPAC, the student may complete only 1 page the first day if the text has a lot of activities or reports, but go on to complete 5 pages the next day.

Long range planning requires some organization. Because the traditional school year originates in the early fall of one year and continues to late spring of the following year, a calendar should be devised that covers this period of time. Approximate beginning and completion dates can be noted on the calendar as well as special occasions such as holidays, vacations and birthdays. Since each LIFEPAC takes 3-4 weeks or eighteen days to complete, it should take about 180 school days to finish a set of ten LIFEPACs. Starting at the beginning school date, mark off eighteen school days on the calendar and that will become the targeted completion date for the first LIFEPAC. Continue marking the calendar until you have established dates for the remaining nine LIFEPACs making adjustments for previously noted holidays and vacations. If all five subjects are being used, the ten established target dates should be the same for the LIFEPACs in each subject.

FORMS

The sample weekly lesson plan and student grading sheet forms are included in this section as teacher support materials and may be duplicated at the convenience of the teacher.

The student grading sheet is provided for those who desire to follow the suggested guidelines for assignment of letter grades found on page 3 of this section. The student's self test scores should be posted as percentage grades. When the LIFEPAC is completed the teacher should average the self test grades, multiply the average by .25 and post the points in the box marked self test points. The LIFEPAC percentage grade should be multiplied by .60 and posted. Next, the teacher should award and post points for written reports and oral work. A report may be any type of written work assigned to the student whether it is a LIFEPAC or additional learning activity. Oral work includes the student's ability to respond orally to questions which may or may not be related to LIFEPAC activities or any type of oral report assigned by the teacher. The points may then be totaled and a final grade entered along with the date that the LIFEPAC was completed.

The Student Record Book which was specifically designed for use with the Alpha Omega curriculum provides space to record weekly progress for one student over a nine week period as well as a place to post self test and LIFEPAC scores. The Student Record Books are available through the current Alpha Omega catalog; however, unlike the enclosed forms these books are not for duplication and should be purchased in sets of four to cover a full academic year.

WEEKLY LESSON PLANNER

Week of:

Subject	Subject	Subject	Subject

Monday

Subject	Subject	Subject	Subject

Tuesday

Subject	Subject	Subject	Subject

Wednesday

Subject	Subject	Subject	Subject

Thursday

Subject	Subject	Subject	Subject

Friday

21

WEEKLY LESSON PLANNER

Week of:

Subject	Subject	Subject	Subject
Monday			
Subject	Subject	Subject	Subject
Tuesday			
Subject	Subject	Subject	Subject
Wednesday			
Subject	Subject	Subject	Subject
Thursday			
Subject	Subject	Subject	Subject
Friday			

Student Name _____   Year _____

Bible

LP #	Self Test Scores by Sections					Self Test Points	LIFEPAC Test	Oral Points	Report Points	Final Grade	Date
	1	2	3	4	5						
01											
02											
03											
04											
05											
06											
07											
08											
09											
10											

History & Geography

LP #	Self Test Scores by Sections					Self Test Points	LIFEPAC Test	Oral Points	Report Points	Final Grade	Date
	1	2	3	4	5						
01											
02											
03											
04											
05											
06											
07											
08											
09											
10											

Language Arts

LP #	Self Test Scores by Sections					Self Test Points	LIFEPAC Test	Oral Points	Report Points	Final Grade	Date
	1	2	3	4	5						
01											
02											
03											
04											
05											
06											
07											
08											
09											
10											

Student Name _____   Year _____

Mathematics

LP #	Self Test Scores by Sections 1	2	3	4	5	Self Test Points	LIFEPAC Test	Oral Points	Report Points	Final Grade	Date
01											
02											
03											
04											
05											
06											
07											
08											
09											
10											

Science

LP #	Self Test Scores by Sections 1	2	3	4	5	Self Test Points	LIFEPAC Test	Oral Points	Report Points	Final Grade	Date
01											
02											
03											
04											
05											
06											
07											
08											
09											
10											

Spelling/Electives

LP #	Self Test Scores by Sections 1	2	3	4	5	Self Test Points	LIFEPAC Test	Oral Points	Report Points	Final Grade	Date
01											
02											
03											
04											
05											
06											
07											
08											
09											
10											

N
O
T
E
S

INSTRUCTIONS FOR LANGUAGE ARTS

The LIFEPAC curriculum from grades two through twelve is structured so that the daily instructional material is written directly into the LIFEPACs. The student is encouraged to read and follow this instructional material in order to develop independent study habits. The teacher should introduce the LIFEPAC to the student, set a required completion schedule, complete teacher checks, be available for questions regarding both content and procedures, administer and grade tests, and develop additional learning activities as desired. Teachers working with several students may schedule their time so that students are assigned to a quiet work activity when it is necessary to spend instructional time with one particular student.

Language arts includes those subjects that develop the students' communication skills. The LIFEPAC approach to combining reading, spelling, penmanship, composition, grammar, speech and literature in a single unit allows the teacher to integrate the study of these various language arts subject areas. The variety and scope of the curriculum may make it difficult for students to complete the required material within the suggested daily scheduled time of forty-five minutes. Spelling, book reports and various forms of composition may need to be completed during the afternoon enrichment period.

Cursive handwriting is introduced in the second grade LIFEPAC 208 with regular practice following in succeeding LIFEPACs. Diacritical markings are defined in the third grade LIFEPAC 304. A pronunciation key including diacritical markings is provided after the vocabulary word lists in all subjects beginning with LIFEPAC 305.

This section of the language arts Teacher's Guide includes the following teacher aids: Index of Concepts, *Book Report Form*, *Books Read Chart*, Suggested and Required Material (supplies), Additional Learning Activities, and LIFEPAC Spelling Tests.

The *Book Report Form* and the *Books Read Chart* may be duplicated for individual student use.

The Index of Concepts is a quick reference guide for the teacher who may be looking for a rule or explanation that applies to a particular concept. It does not identify each use of the concept in the various LIFEPACs. The concepts change by grade level with the emphasis on phonics and reading skills changing to spelling and grammar for the older students.

Spelling tests contained in the handbook are final spelling tests and should be administered with each Language Arts LIFEPAC test. Many words such as `piece' and `peace' are dependent on meaning for correct spelling. By placing the spelling words in sentences, the spelling tests simplify the teacher's work of properly presenting the correct words from the LIFEPAC spelling lists.

The materials section refers only to LIFEPAC materials and does not include materials which may be needed for the additional learning activities. Additional learning activities provide a change from the daily school routine, encourage the student's interest in learning and may be used as a reward for good study habits.

Concept	LIFEPAC	Section	Concept	LIFEPAC	Section
Abbreviations	805	1	Literary Forms		
			autobiography	806	3
Antonyms	804	1	essay	803	2
			fiction/nonfiction	808	3
Capitalization	805	1			
			Morphemes	801	1
Categorizing/classifying	801	1			
analogy	801	1	News Sources	808	3
Composition			Paragraph Structure	807	2
business letter	808	1	(coherence, unity,		
essay	803	2	concluding sentence,		
personal letter	808	1	patterns, purposes,		
theme	807	3	topic sentence)		
Critical Reading Skills			Parts of Speech		
author's bias	807	1	adjectives	802	2,3
evaluating words	807	1	adverbs	802	2,3
evaluating statistics	808	3	conjunctions	806	2
fact/opinion	808	3	(coordinate, correlative,		
false reasoning	807	1	subordinate)		
			interjections	801	2
Development of English			nouns		
dialects	802	1	concrete/abstract	810	4
etymology	808	1	possessive	805	1
history of English	806	1	proper/common	802	2
language families	802	1	pronouns	802	2
standardization	809	1	verbs		
			auxiliary (helping)	802	2
Dictionary - history/use	804	1	contractions	805	1
			tense	802	2
English Usage					
standard/nonstandard	804	3	Prefixes	801	1
Following Directions	801	2	Propaganda Techniques	807	1
	804	1			
			Punctuation	803	1
				805	1
Grammar Errors	809	2			
			Root Words	801	1
Homonyms	805	3			
			Semantic Meaning	801	1
Inflections	801	1			

Concept	LIFEPAC	Section	Concept	LIFEPAC	Section
Sentence Structure					
appositives	806	2			
clauses	806	2			
coordination	806	2			
phrases					
adjective/adverb	802	3			
parenthetic	803	1			
participial	806	2			
prepositional	806	2			
sentence	810	1			
sentence errors	810	1			
sentence types	803	1			
subject/predicate	810	1			
subordination	806	2			
Speech					
Biblical standards	810	2			
oral reports (pentad)	809	3			
speaking qualities	805	2			
Suffixes	801	1			
Syllables/Accents	804	2			
Synonyms	804	1			
Thesaurus	804	1			
Writing Numbers and Figures	805	1			

BOOK REPORT FORM

Title_____   Your Name _____

Author_____   Date _____

Illustrator_____   Principal Characters _____

Number of Pages_____   _____

Copyright Date_____   _____

Fiction or Nonfiction_____   Setting _____

Summary: A summary gives the important events of a story or book. It skips most of the details but a few make the report more interesting. The summary should be written in complete sentences.

_____

_____

_____

_____

_____

_____

_____

_____

_____

_____

_____

_____

Tell why you did or did not like the book.

_____

_____

_____

_____

_____

_____

_____

_____

BOOKS READ

Title:	Title:	Title:	Title:
Author:	Author:	Author:	Author:
Date:	Date:	Date:	Date:
Title:	Title:	Title:	Title:
Author:	Author:	Author:	Author:
Date:	Date:	Date:	Date:
Title:	Title:	Title:	Title:
Author:	Author:	Author:	Author:
Date:	Date:	Date:	Date:
Title:	Title:	Title:	Title:
Author:	Author:	Author:	Author:
Date:	Date:	Date:	Date:
Title:	Title:	Title:	Title:
Author:	Author:	Author:	Author:
Date:	Date:	Date:	Date:
Title:	Title:	Title:	Title:
Author:	Author:	Author:	Author:
Date:	Date:	Date:	Date:
Title:	Title:	Title:	Title:
Author:	Author:	Author:	Author:
Date:	Date:	Date:	Date:
Title:	Title:	Title:	Title:
Author:	Author:	Author:	Author:
Date:	Date:	Date:	Date:
Title:	Title:	Title:	Title:
Author:	Author:	Author:	Author:
Date:	Date:	Date:	Date:

Materials Needed for LIFEPAC

Required: Suggested:
None   dictionary
                                   a mirror

Additional Learning Activities

Section I Improving Your Reading

1. Discuss these questions.
   a. What is a definition for the word *communication*?
   b. What are context clues?
   c. What are some ways you can unlock words?
   d. What are inflections?
   e. What are morphemes?
   f. What is a free morpheme?
   g. What is a bound morpheme?
   h. What are comparative and superlative degrees in adjectives?
   i. What is semantic meaning?
   j. What do we mean by categorizing, or classifying?
   k. What is an analogy? (Form the first part of an analogy and let students finish it.)

2. Explain how you can take a word and create a new word. Write a word on the board and see how many new words the student(s) can create from this root word.

3. List ten categories on the chalkboard and have the students number on a sheet from one to eighteen. Have the students keep three categories in mind and write a list of six items that would fit under each category. Have the students exchange papers and by looking at the list on the board decide what the three categories are and arrange items under the correct categories.

4. Have a student write a short story that includes many interjections.

5. Students may find weather reports, news or sports articles, or advertisements and underline the roots, circle the prefixes, and draw a box around the suffixes. See who can find a sentence containing the most words formed from prefixes and suffixes.

Section II Following Directions

1. Discuss these questions.
   a. Why is it important to know how to follow instructions?
   b. What is the most important listening courtesy?
   c. How does remembering the sequence help you?
   d. What should you remember when writing instructions?
   e. What should you remember when taking notes?

2. Set up a listening activity. Prepare directions for performing a task, starting with a relatively simple set of instructions. Read these to the student(s). Do not repeat any steps. See which students were able to follow directions without any problems. These students can help slower ones learn to follow directions. Some art or craft books contain instructions for various projects: making paper mâché, quilling, or origami (paper folding). Example:
   1. Take a square piece of paper (about 9" x 9").
   2. Fold the square once diagonally to form a triangle.
   3. Turn the triangle so that the longest side is on the bottom.
   4. Fold the bottom under about one-third.
   5. Now fold back each side forming a pentagon shape (do not worry about the extra points behind).
   6. Now fold the center triangle back. What have you made? A cat's head.
3. Students may take turns presenting directions to the class. Suggestions: how to make cookies, how to play golf, how to drive a car, how to ski, and so forth.
4. Have the student write down the directions from the school to his house and share them with a classmate who doesn't know where he lives.

Section III Communication Without Words
1. Discuss these questions.
   a. What are some methods of nonverbal communication?
   b. How can movements of the hands carry messages?
   c. What silent messages can your posture carry?
   d. How do facial expressions carry messages?
   e. How does your appearance carry a message?
   f. Do your eyes carry messages? What kind of messages can your eyes give?
   g. What are interjections?
   h. How do deaf people communicate?
2. Have a group recite Psalm 1 using sign language.
3. Divide the students into groups, and let each group choose something to pantomime. Example: a family having their picture taken.
4. Have a student look up information on how any one of the following people uses sign language: the deaf, police, military, bicyclists.
5. Students may read about various deaf people and report to the class.
6. Students may want to interview a policeman, military person, telegraph operator, referee or umpire, or other user of signals and report to the class.

Materials Needed for LIFEPAC

Required:

Suggested:
English-to-French or English-to-
   Spanish dictionary
some pictorial magazines
scissors
paste

Additional Learning Activities

Section I History of the English Language

1. Discuss these questions:
   a. Why do you use the English language to communicate?
   b. What is one of the most important tools of language?
2. Ask students to communicate a message to you, using no words.
3. Learn some old ballads (mountain). Discuss the meaning and dialect used.
4. Read the book *Christy* by Catherine Marshall. This story contains quite a few examples of mountain dialect. Write a book report or present a short sketch or read a passage in dialect to the class.
5. Make a bulletin board tracing the roots and development of language. See the Language Tree in Section I of the LIFEPAC.
6. Look in the dictionary and find the origins of the first five spelling words on page 9 of the LIFEPAC.

Section II Classification of Words

1. From the LIFEPAC, write the sentences of the first test for nouns on the blackboard. Write a list of various types of words beside it. Let students take turns determining if a word is a noun by substituting it in the blanks.
2. Read a short paragraph to the student(s), substituting the same nonsense word for each noun (example: *scurtsbrug*). See if anyone can identify the source of the paragraph or the idea it is expressing.
3. Give each group of students a simple sentence (The boy ate.) and see which group can build an *interesting*, long sentence using the most words in a limited time.
4. Let students set up questions. One group asks, what is a four-letter noun for something that is thrown? Other group answers, a ball. The object of the game is to frame a question that can be answered in only one guess. Students must give the part of speech.
5. Have a poster contest. Let each student design a colorful, well organized poster describing one of the word classes. The poster may be serious or humorous, using any media.

Section III Using Our Language

1. Choose a story or poem using vivid adjectives and adverbs, and read it to the student(s).
2. Write a simple noun on the board. See how many vivid adjectives and adverbs the student(s) can furnish.
3. Let each group describe an object to the other group and see if the second group can guess it. The describing group must use two adjectives each turn to describe the object. If the second group does not guess the answer in three tries, they must try another word. When the second group answers in three guesses or less, they may describe an object to the other group.
4. Let several students make up a story with a particular mood—humor, mystery, and so on—determined by adjectives. One person starts telling the story, builds up to an interesting description (…and there in the doorway, dripping wet, eyes glaring, teeth chattering, stood _____ .) and stops for the next student to supply the noun and continue the story.
5. Write your own poem, story, or paragraph, using vivid adjectives and adverbs.
6. Draw a picture to illustrate a descriptive passage from a poem or a book.

Materials needed for LIFEPAC

Required:
None

Suggested:
older magazines containing short,
    acceptable articles
scissors
red ink
magazines or books containing short,
    formal (acceptable) essays

Additional Learning Activities

Section I Punctuation

1. Ask this question: What would conversation be like if we used no punctuation?
2. Try an experiment: Ask each student to read several lines from a book without indicating the punctuation.
3. One group should make up a series of sentences. Another group should draw a large punctuation mark on 1/4 sheet of paper. As group *A* reads its sentences aloud, group *B* holds up the appropriate punctuation mark. Five points are given for each correct mark of punctuation and five are subtracted for each incorrect mark. When group *B* has twenty-five points, the groups change places. The first team to score fifty points wins.
4. Divide the class into groups and have them make up jingles or slogans about punctuation. Example: Are your sentences tired and worn out? Do they fade out before they are finished? If so, you need exclamation points! They add zest to your thoughts.
5. Write a recipe for using punctuation.
6. Find a famous quotation in a source such as Bartlett's *Familiar Quotations*, the Bible, or a Shakespearean play. On a sheet of plain white or pastel paper neatly letter the quotation and its punctuation marks. You may design an attractive border and display examples of various types of punctuation in the classroom.
7. Find a book written by Charles Dickens, Jane Austin, or Sir Walter Scott. Notice the punctuation used in the book. Compare it with the punctuation used in a newspaper article or other current publication.

Section II Literature

1. Discuss the reasons for and benefits of pain after students have read the first essay in Section II.
2. Try to find Biblical references to pain and suffering, read these passages, and discuss the way a Christian should react to pain and suffering.
3. Find an essay recommended by your parents, teacher, or librarian. Read it and write a short report about it, telling what kind of essay it is and how the author supports his main idea.

Materials Needed for LIFEPAC

Required: Suggested:
None   dictionary
                                    The Holy Bible, King James Version

Additional Learning Activities

Section I Words and How to Use Them

1. Take the students to a public library or a college library so that they may examine a variety of dictionaries. Arrange this field trip with the librarian in advance. If a trip is not feasible invite a librarian to visit the class and explain various types of dictionaries to the class.

2. Borrow, rent, or buy filmstrips or other audio visual materials about the library.

3. Play Thesaurus Scrabble. If you do not have a game, you can make a temporary one from cardboard or a more durable one from linoleum or wood squares (about 1"). You will need about five squares for each consonant and about ten squares for each vowel. Start by choosing seven squares each. The first player who can form a word should do so. He should consult a thesaurus or a dictionary. The longer the word, the higher the score. Let each consonant count four points and each vowel three (you may vary point values to allow seldom-used letters such as x, z, and q to have higher point values). If the next player cannot make a word to connect to the first word, he must draw another square and either make a word or discard. Play continues until a prayer scores one hundred or until letters run out. You might like to award extra points for unusual words. *Variation* : Play Bible Scrabble, using names, places, and words from the Bible.

4. Find a famous quotation. Using a thesaurus or dictionary, substitute synonyms for several of the major words and rewrite it. You might like to read some of these to the class to see if anyone recognizes the original *Variation*: Try substituting antonyms.

Section II Pronouncing Words

1. Write some difficult pronunciations on the board, indicated by diacritical marks and see how well the student(s) performs.
2. Direct the student(s) to make its own pronunciation key using Bible words. Write suggestions on the board, choose the best words, and make copies for future use.
3. Have a pronunciation bee. Look up the pronunciation for twenty-five or thirty difficult words. Write each word on one side of a flash card (3" x 5" paper or cardboard) and the correct pronunciation on the other side. Ask another group to pronounce each word. Each person who misses must go to the end of the line. The person at the front of the line is the champion. Then let that group look up words and the other group pronounce them.
4. Find a Bible verse containing several hard-to-pronounce words. Look up each word in a dictionary and mark it. Now read the verse to another person to try out the pronunciations.

Section III Using Words Correctly

1. Write a paragraph using nonstandard English. Discuss each error with the class, letting individual students correct each error.
2. Make a slang dictionary. Write the terms commonly used in your school and define them in standard English.
3. Locate nonstandard usage in advertisements and rewrite them, using standard English.

Materials Needed for LIFEPAC

Required:
None

Suggested:
encyclopedia or a biographical dictionary
old magazines or newspapers
scissors
paste
literature anthology or history book
The Holy Bible, King James Version, or textbook,
newspaper, magazine, or other approved book

Additional Learning Activities

Section I Written Language

1. Make a list of common names, words, or terms (example: the fifty states) having set abbreviations. Play an abbreviation game. Each player in turn picks a folded paper with a word written on it. He has five seconds to provide the correct abbreviation. If he does he gets five points; if not, he loses five points. The first player with twenty-five points wins.

2. Pupil could write up articles about school activities getting various viewpoints from different people. These viewpoints should be quoted and written correctly in the articles.

Section II Spoken Language

1. Discuss various hobbies enjoyed by students. Have each student choose a hobby to explain to the class in a short two- to three-minute speech. Using the check Section II of the LIFEPAC, or one of your own, evaluate each student's performance.

2. Find and prepare a list of rules about speaking from various Bible verses.

3. Read a book about a famous person. Select one incident from this book and relate it to a friend, again being sure to use all the qualities of a good speaker.

Section III Correct Usage

1. Discuss often confused word pairs with the class and see if the group can think of other words to add to the list.

2. Play a word game. Prepare a list of nouns, verbs, adjectives, and adverbs. On 3″ x 5″ cards write *synonym, antonym,* and *homonym* (one word per card). One person should be the word-caller. He should choose a person and call out the word. That person then must pick up one of the cards (which are face down) and give the caller a synonym, antonym, or homonym (as indicated by the card) for that word. He should have five or ten seconds to answer or lose his turn. The person giving the most correct answers wins.

3. Find a paragraph in an approved book and rewrite it substituting synonyms for as many words as possible. Compare the two paragraphs. Do they both say the same thing or have you chosen words with slightly different connotations?

Materials needed for LIFEPAC

Required:
None

Suggested:
The Holy Bible, King James
  Version
World Book Encyclopedia or any
  other available
  encyclopedia
a copy of *Beowulf*, "The Seafarer,"
  some Anglo-Saxon Riddles,
  or "The Wanderer."

Additional Learning Activities

Section I The Nature of Language

1. Have a class discussion about epics. Explain the qualities of the epic and the epic hero. Ask the student(s) to consider whether or not an epic could be written about the modern world.
2. Find a copy of the legend of Paul Bunyan or any other story about a hero. Discuss this hero's personality and deeds and compare them with Beowulf's.
3. Choose a person from fairly modern history and make up an epic story about one of his deeds. Tell it to another group. Consider this question—Does it seem suitably serious or is it exaggerated?
4. Students who have access to a good library may want to look up *mock-epic* or *mock-heroic* to learn its meaning. Some students may want to write a mock-epic.
5. Artistic students may want to draw some scenes from any early period of English history or from any of the literature they have read.
6. Copy a few words or a sentence or two in Old or Middle English on art paper and design an appropriate border.

Section II The Construction of Sentences

1. Write various types of sentences on the board or on work sheets. Have students identify coordinate and subordinate elements, essential and nonessential elements and the various types of conjunctions and other words used to introduce or join clauses.
2. Choose a simple book (perhaps one suitable for about third grade level). Rewrite or combine some of the sentences by using subordination or coordination.
3. Make posters to illustrate the use of coordination or subordination. Display in class.

Section III The Autobiography

1. Discuss the themes of both autobiographical sketches with the class. Bring out the various elements of autobiography and the way the author revealed them.
2. Dramatize the turning point in the "Flight to the South Pole." Discuss the feelings each person must have had at that time.
3. Pretend you were along with Admiral Byrd's expedition. Write an autobiographical diary entry or letter about some part of your trip.

Materials Needed for LIFEPAC

Required:
None

Suggested:
dictionary
newspapers and magazines

Additional Learning Activities

Section I Critical Reading

1. Find examples of several slanted articles and read portions to the student(s). Discuss the techniques used by the author.
2. Check student's ability to determine word meaning through the context by writing sentences containing unfamiliar words and "hints" to meaning. For example: "The weaver's *adroitness* amazed the apprentice."
3. Prepare a list of reasons your group supports or opposes some issue or movement (prayer in school, twelve-month school year, higher age for drivers' licenses, etc.) Let another group read over your reasons and evaluate them. Did you use facts or opinions? Did you use logic or false reasoning? Did you use any propaganda techniques? If so, which ones?
4. Find a copy of Thomas Paine's "Common Sense" or any other approved essay. Look over parts of this article and see if you can identify examples of fact, opinion, propaganda, or logical or misleading reasoning.
5. Find a modern editorial from a newspaper. What techniques or persuasion does the writer use?
6. Look up Thomas Paine or the author whose work you read in the first activity. What are his credentials?

Section II Paragraphs

1. Write a poorly organized paragraph on work sheets or on the board. Ask students to analyze it and rewrite it.
2. Find examples of different types of paragraphs in books or magazines. Analyze these paragraphs.
3. Find a sample paragraph and circle all transitional words. Underline the topic sentence. Cross out any sentences that seem unrelated to the topic sentence.

Section III Composition

1. If you have a projector, or can make a copy of a well organized paper, show the class the necessary elements of a composition.
2. Read several good introductory and concluding paragraphs to the class. Ask them, "What makes these paragraphs good?"
3. Make up a poor introductory or concluding paragraph. Ask students to improve it.
4. Make up sentence fragments and run-on sentences. Give these "sentences" to another group to identify and to correct.
5. Have a spelling bee.
6. Outline a well organized paper and write a thesis for it.

Materials Needed for LIFEPAC

Required: Suggested:
None   envelopes, preferably 4 1/8" x 9 1/2"
                                   a decibel meter
                                   dictionary
                                   Bible stories told in narrative from a book
                                       of photographs, a magazine, or a film-
                                       strip (Edward Steichen's marvelous
                                       work, *The Family of Man*, would work
                                       beautifully)
                                   The Holy Bible, King James Version
                                   encyclopedia
                                   various newspapers and magazines
                                   local newspaper, one for each student

Additional Learning Activities

Section I Writing Letters

1. Discuss writing letters. Have each student contribute ideas for writing a class letter to a sick classmate or a thank-you letter for some service or program presented to the class or school.

2. Each group should choose some state department to write asking for information about their state. Write to the Department of Agriculture, the Department of Transportation, the Department of Education, the Game and Fish Department, the Highway Patrol, the State Health Services, the Library Archives and Public Records Department, the Solar Energy Research Commission, the Office of Tourism, or any other state agency. The teacher should read and approve all letters before they are sent.

3. Find out if your library has books of collected letters to or from famous people.

Section II. Developing Listening Skills

1. Demonstrate the use of a decibel meter if you have access to one. Use the meter to measure various sounds in and around the classroom. Discuss the effect of high decibel levels on hearing and on emotional stability.

2. Make flash cards using a number of different figures of speech. Drill the students on recognition of phrases (i.e., what figure of speech is found in "he sleeps like a log") and on making up their own figures of speech (i.e., show a card with "metaphor" on it, and ask for a metaphor about Joshua at Jericho, as in "Joshua was as determined as a...").

3. Divide students into groups of two. Give each pair the task of telling each other some embarrassing or meaningful incident they have experienced. The listener must use active listening skills. Afterward, ask students to discuss how they felt about having an active listener to whom they could tell something personal. How did the listeners feel?

4. Students should keep a record of the gestures they use daily in school (raised hand, shrugged shoulders, and so forth). They should record descriptions of these gestures and why they give particular meanings to certain gestures, expressions, and body postures.

5. Circulate a picture around the group. Each person should write down his or her interpretation of what's happening in the picture. Compare the various interpretations.

6. Play a game of "telephone." Start a story at one side of the room; each student whispers what they hear to the next person. Compare the beginning story with the garbled version that emerges at the end. Discuss the breakdowns in communication that led to this result.

7. Students can take photographs of people expressing various nonverbal messages and show the slides or snapshots to the class to see if they can recognize the messages. Students may collect pictures from approved magazines or newspapers and label with appropriate titles or captions.

8. Survey some political speeches as reported in your local newspaper for the use of "code words." Translate the code words into their actual meanings.

9. Make a poster showing the mechanism of the human ear. Show on the poster why high decibel levels can cause permanent injury to a person's hearing.

Section III Reading Nonfiction

1. Set up a shelf of assorted fiction and nonfiction books. Ask students to separate the fiction from the nonfiction. Make a game of it by timing each person as he goes through the exercise.

2. Collect some examples of propaganda. Mount the clippings or copies of the clippings and circulate them among the students. Ask them to use logical thinking to detect the nature and purpose of the propaganda.

3. Take students to a library. If they have never used this library, arrange in advance for the librarian to explain the use and location of the library's research materials. Give each of them a treasure hunt sheet which directs them to find such items as:
   (a) a primary source on the Cuban Missile Crisis
   (b) a secondary source on the life of St. Paul
   (c) a reference source that can tell them how far it is from Damascus to Rome
   (d) a magazine article on inflation; and so forth.

4. Write letters to public officials (school administration, city council, state legislators, etc.) asking them to help get some project through that is important to your community.

5. Go out with other students to interview people in your community about some important issue—an election, a church matter, the need for better recreational facilities, or whatever is appropriate in your area. Plan your interviews so that you cover a good cross-section of the local populace.

6. Write a letter to the editor of your local paper about a matter about which you feel strongly.

7. Make a collection of different types of newspaper stories. Identify the five *W's* and the *H* in each story.

8. Write a "mini" research paper. As an initial experience in compiling a research type paper, this assignment should be given after an adequate explanation and tour of the library facilities. Students should choose or be assigned general topics for which adequate information exists. Choice may come from current events or history, Bible, or science (for example, Martin Luther; George Washington). Students should then go to the card catalog to find available books about their topics. If the library has some bound periodicals, students can be shown how to use the *Readers' Guide* to find information. Work with the librarian in providing sufficient help and instruction for locating various types of information. Don't forget newspapers and news magazines. Encourage students to use at least three sources (depending upon availability) and take notes from them. Explain the difference between copying and paraphrasing. Students should list a simple, alphabetized bibliography at the end of the paper, citing the usual publication information and pages used. Some teachers require a rough outline, rough draft, and final draft, checking each one and guiding student progress.

Materials Needed for LIFEPAC

Required: Suggested:
None   any unabridged dictionary
                                          a newspaper

Additional Learning Activities

Section I English is Alive

1. Invite an English person to speak to the class, explaining the differences in United States English and English as spoken in England.
2. Invite a person who has come from another country and who originally spoke a foreign language to speak to the class about unique features of English.
3. Find information about a certain period of English history and present information to the class.
4. Learn more about the early inhabitants or conquerors of England. Look up William the Conqueror, Geoffrey Chaucer, Stonehenge, the Celts, or the Anglo-Saxons.

Section II Good Grammar Makes Good Sense

1. Write on the board some sentences containing shifts in person, mood, and tense. Ask students to correct them.
2. Keep a journal of all double negatives and dangling modifiers you hear for a week. You could draw and label cartoons of these errors to share with the student(s). Do not reveal the identity of any person making these errors.

Section III An Oral Report Should Be Organized

1. Invite a person who writes for a local newspaper to explain the necessary elements for a news story.
2. Invite a person who has taken an interesting trip to a foreign country (if possible). Ask that person to present pictures and information, allowing the student(s) to ask prepared questions based on the pentad. If the guest presents such a comprehensive talk that the students have few questions, ask them to fill in the answers to the pentad as an outline.
3. Have five students decide upon a common topic to research. Each student should concentrate on one question of the pentad. Students may present their report to another group or to the whole class.
4. Write a short but complete paper about one of the reports presented in class. The paper should have a thesis in the introduction, a main body, and a conclusion. Check this paper using the same criteria as for the Extended Writing Assignment.

Materials Needed for LIFEPAC

Required:

The entire Language Arts 800 series should be made available for student review and clarification purposes.

Suggested:

The Holy Bible, King James Version
dictionary
thesaurus
cardboard or heavy paper
mirror
ruler
newspaper or approved news magazine
magazine or book of formal and informal essays
some approved autobiographies

Additional Learning Activities

Section I Language

1. Have a dictionary race. Write a word on the board. The first student to find and define the word orally may choose the next word.

2. Each group should prepare a parts of speech game. Each person should have a card (8" x 10"). Divide the card into thirty squares (1" each). Across the top write the numbers a, 2, 3, 4, and 5, one per square. In the other squares write the parts of speech—repeating and rearranging—until the card has been filled. Make each card slightly different. Each card should have a free square in the center. One person should write a five word sentence on the board or on a piece of paper. Each person, in turn, will identify the part of speech of each word in the sentence—in order. He should place a marker (a small piece of colored paper, a dried bean, button, or other object) on one square containing that part of speech. The first person to cover an entire row—horizontally, vertically, or diagonally—wins.

3. Each student should choose one commonly used word, look it up in a thesaurus, and write down all the possible synonyms. These synonyms may be collected into a class thesaurus.

Section II Communication

1. Start the students in pantomime and nonverbal communication by trying one or all of these activities:

   a. Form a circle and pass around an invisible jar of pickles. It's hard to open and should stay the same size as it is "passed" around.

   b. Have students be parts of a machine. Ask one student to start the machine with some kind of sound and motion. Point to students one at a time to join the machine and add a new part. The first motions should be easily repeated many times or the machine will not "last" through the last student.

   c. Try a make-believe ball game. Have the students toss a ball back and forth in a circle. Have them watch for motions that match the sending action to the receiving action. Tell them to watch the "size" of the ball.

2. Set up a newspaper. Each student should choose or be assigned a particular area of responsibility (preparing editorials, preparing artwork or cartoons related to school news, reporting school events, interviewing outstanding or interesting people involved with your school, etc.). Each student should choose an editor to assign stories, compile material, and assure that deadlines are met. A strong English student might form the editorial group, responsible for writing editorials, for choosing materials to be used, and for checking the grammar and mechanics of materials submitted.

3. Students may present a pantomime to a group or to the entire class. Possible subjects might include these:
   a. a Sunday drive in an old jalopy,
   b. a robot; overworked, bumbling, or moody,
   c. puppets revolt,
   d. walking through the park with bubble gum,
   e. the huge dog,
   f. the one that got away,
   g. a new pizza parlor; or
   h. the haircut.

4. Students may prepare and present a short speech. Suggested topics might include these:
   a. five ways to kill a fly,
   b. some melting words about chocolate,
   c. the best or worst thing about school,
   d. one favorite person I knew,
   e. the first time I tasted broccoli,
   f. what to do when you're tired of the gum,
   g. why I became a Christian,
   h. how we can bring others to Christ,
   i. my favorite meal,
   j. changing a tire,
   k. the next time you're really hungry,
   l. you should see my pet _____ ,
   m. the most exciting job in the world must be _____, or
   n. how to make a sad person smile.
   Remind students to have a purpose.

Section III Reading

1. Prepare a list of statements—some based on fact, others based on opinion. Ask students to determine which statement is which.
2. Prepare some out of sequence activities. Duplicate these and ask students to rearrange them in proper sequence.
3. Have a spelling bee over all the words in the LIFEPAC.

4. The teacher should provide or recommend a good essay (possibly one by James Thurber or Stephen Leacock). Students should read the essay and determine its purpose. If it contains any unfamiliar words, students should try to unlock the meaning by the techniques required in this LIFEPAC.
5. Students should list and explain three elements of an autobiography.
6. Choose an episode from your life and write a short autobiographical sketch. The elements of autobiography should be included in this sketch.

LIFEPAC TEST

1.	siege	The enemy laid <u>siege</u> to the fortress.	siege
2.	freight	The <u>freight</u> truck was fully loaded.	freight
3.	mischievous	The <u>mischievous</u> child had hidden the book.	mischievous
4.	sieve	Use a <u>sieve</u> to remove the lumps from the flour.	sieve
5.	neither	<u>Neither</u> Beth nor Patti went to school yesterday.	neither
6.	reign	The queen will <u>reign</u> for a year.	reign
7.	surveillance	The suspects are under police <u>surveillance</u>.	surveillance
8.	yield	Those tomato plants usually <u>yield</u> three bushels.	yield
9.	efficient	The secretary is very <u>efficient</u>.	efficient
10.	leisure	I like to play tennis in my <u>leisure</u> time.	leisure
11.	friend	Valarie's best <u>friend</u> is Heather.	friend
12.	perceive	Arnold cannot <u>perceive</u> the difference between fact and fiction.	perceive
13.	heirloom	That gold locket is an <u>heirloom.</u>	heirloom
14.	medieval	The <u>medieval</u> castle was dark and gloomy.	medieval
15.	niece	Jan's <u>niece</u> is three years old.	niece
16.	priest	The <u>priest</u> visited the hospital daily.	priest
17.	prelude	The <u>prelude</u> was performed beautifully.	prelude
18.	inedible	A pencil is <u>inedible</u>, so take it out of your mouth.	inedible
19.	foreshadow	To <u>foreshadow</u> means to warn of an event to come.	foreshadow
20.	biennial	The celebration is <u>biennial.</u>	biennial
21.	inarticulate	Embarrassment made him <u>inarticulate</u>.	inarticulate
22.	transcontinental	Edward wants to take a <u>transcontinental</u> journey.	transcontinental
23.	preeminent	Doctor Wilson is a <u>preeminent</u> philosopher.	preeminent
24.	prehistoric	Those bones may be <u>prehistoric</u>.	prehistoric
25.	antonym	Cold is the <u>antonym</u> for hot.	antonym
26.	descend	The bride will <u>descend</u> the stairs at three o'clock.	descend
27.	departure	Our <u>departure</u> time should be changed.	departure
28.	reiterate	Would you <u>reiterate</u> your reasons, please?	reiterate
29.	aftermath	The authorities inspected the <u>aftermath</u> to the storm.	aftermath
30.	antediluvian	The time in which Cain and Abel lived was the <u>antediluvian.</u>	antediluvian
31.	involuntary	Breathing is an <u>involuntary</u> action.	involuntary

LIFEPAC TEST cont…

32.	transmission	My car needs a new transmission.	transmission
33.	expulsion	Benny's fight resulted in his expulsion from school.	expulsion
34.	scientifically	He learned to investigate scientifically.	scientifically
35.	responsibility	You have a responsibility to God.	responsibility
36.	reference	Jack is the new reference librarian.	reference
37.	Christianity	Christianity has had a great influence in my life.	Christianity
38.	inaccessible	The campground was almost inaccessible.	inaccessible
39.	Biblical	The Biblical account of Moses is a favorite of mine.	Biblical
40.	marriage	Marriage should be a lasting relationship.	marriage
41.	happiness	His smile indicated his happiness.	happiness
42.	argument	Marty's argument was sound.	argument

ALTERNATE LIFEPAC TEST

1.	<u>seize</u>	He had to <u>seize</u> the rope.	<u>seize</u>
2.	<u>brief</u>	The lecture was <u>brief</u> and informative.	<u>brief</u>
3.	<u>reign</u>	The prince may <u>reign</u> when he is older.	<u>reign</u>
4.	<u>field</u>	A <u>field</u> of wheat was being harvested.	<u>field</u>
5.	<u>fiend</u>	Is Satan a <u>fiend?</u>	<u>fiend</u>
6.	<u>heinous</u>	Murder is a <u>heinous</u> crime.	<u>heinous</u>
7.	<u>mischievous</u>	The <u>mischievous</u> child hid behind the door.	<u>mischievous</u>
8.	<u>grief</u>	His <u>grief</u> was overpowering.	<u>grief</u>
9.	<u>neither</u>	<u>Neither</u> rain nor sleet will stop the mail.	<u>neither</u>
10.	<u>kaleidoscope</u>	The <u>kaleidoscope</u> image looked like a stained glass window.	<u>kaleidoscope</u>
11.	<u>neigh</u>	The <u>neigh</u> of horses could be heard across the pasture.	<u>neigh</u>
12.	<u>sleigh</u>	The <u>sleigh</u> bells jingled through the streets.	<u>sleigh</u>
13.	<u>height</u>	He has grown two inches in <u>height</u> this year.	<u>height</u>
14.	<u>pierce</u>	I do not want to <u>pierce</u> my ears.	<u>pierce</u>
15.	<u>lei</u>	She placed a beautiful <u>lei</u> around Jan's neck.	<u>lei</u>
16.	<u>view</u>	The <u>view</u> of the canyon was breathtaking.	<u>view</u>
17.	<u>anti-intellectual</u>	The Romantics tended to be <u>anti-intellectual</u>.	<u>anti-intellectual</u>
18.	<u>trans-Atlantic</u>	Have you ever received a <u>trans-Atlantic</u> telephone call?	<u>trans-Atlantic</u>
19.	<u>non-English</u>	A <u>non-English</u> word should be italicized.	<u>non-English</u>
20.	<u>unfriendly</u>	Gregory was very <u>unfriendly</u>.	<u>unfriendly</u>
21.	<u>pre-shrunk</u>	This blouse is supposed to be <u>pre-shrunk</u>.	<u>pre-shrunk</u>
22.	<u>antislavery</u>	The underground railroad was a part of the <u>antislavery</u> movement.	<u>antislavery</u>
23.	<u>nonmember</u>	The fee for a <u>nonmember</u> is higher.	<u>nonmember</u>
24.	<u>nonnuclear</u>	The new submarine is <u>nonnuclear</u>.	<u>nonnuclear</u>
25.	<u>interrupt</u>	Don't <u>interrupt</u> me when I'm working.	<u>interrupt</u>
26.	<u>subterranean</u>	The <u>subterranean</u> mineshaft collapsed.	<u>subterranean</u>
27.	<u>semiannual</u>	Our <u>semiannual</u> flower festival was canceled.	<u>semiannual</u>
28.	<u>honorable</u>	Stealing is not an <u>honorable</u> pastime.	<u>honorable</u>
29.	<u>heaviness</u>	The <u>heaviness</u> of the package was surprising.	<u>heaviness</u>
30.	<u>picnicker</u>	An ant crawled across the foot of the <u>picnicker</u>.	<u>picnicker</u>
31.	<u>referral</u>	His employer gave him a <u>referral</u>.	<u>referral</u>
32.	<u>reference</u>	May I list you as a <u>reference?</u>	<u>reference</u>

ALTERNATE LIFEPAC TEST cont...

33.	duly	The invoices have been <u>duly</u> processed.	duly
34.	portable	My <u>portable</u> radio is not working.	portable
35.	defamation	The newspaper was sued for <u>defamation</u> of character.	defamation
36.	spherical	The earth is approximately <u>spherical</u> in shape.	spherical
37.	fabulous	Marco Polo must have had some <u>fabulous</u> adventures.	fabulous
38.	inspiration	The psalms are a source of <u>inspiration</u> for many people.	inspiration
39.	indelibly	The message of the Ten Commandments was written <u>indelibly</u> on stone tablets.	indelibly
40.	omitting	I am always <u>omitting</u> commas in compound sentences.	omitting
41.	scientifically	Let's approach this problem <u>scientifically</u>.	scientifically
42.	courageous	Daniel was a <u>courageous</u> man.	courageous
43.	biennial	Carrots are <u>biennial</u> plants.	biennial
44.	aforementioned	The <u>aforementioned</u> chapter also discusses prepositions.	aforementioned
45.	reiterate	Be certain you <u>reiterate</u> the points you made earlier.	reiterate
46.	antonym	Hot is an <u>antonym</u> of cold.	antonym
47.	departure	Her <u>departure</u> from the country grieved her parents.	departure
48.	perceive	I <u>perceive</u> that he means more than he says.	perceive
49.	priest	The <u>priest</u> baptized the girl and her baby sister.	priest

LIFEPAC TEST

1.	analytical	Richard has an analytical mind.	analytical
2.	language	Joann wanted to study a foreign language.	language
3.	separate	It is tricky to separate egg yolks.	separate
4.	phenomenon	A solar eclipse is an interesting phenomenon.	phenomenon
5.	distinguish	You should distinguish between primary and secondary colors.	distinguish
6.	linguist	One linguist studied seven languages.	linguist
7.	concept	That concept is hard to explain.	concept
8.	symbol	The cross is a symbol for Christ's love and sacrifice.	symbol
9.	philologist	A philologist studies language.	philologist
10.	identify	He was able to identify the thief.	identify
11.	civilization	The Mayan civilization was very interesting.	civilization
12.	expression	You should have seen the expression on his face!	expression
13.	signal	They will signal the plane to land.	signal
14.	descendant	Edward was a descendant of the duke.	descendant
15.	isolated	George lives on an isolated island.	isolated
16.	dialect	The island people use an unusual dialect.	dialect
17.	auxiliary	"Have" is an auxiliary verb.	auxiliary
18.	bicycle	Karen's bicycle needs painting.	bicycle
19.	categorize	How do you categorize ideas?	categorize
20.	racquet	I bought a new tennis racquet yesterday.	racquet
21.	heavily	It was raining heavily last night.	heavily
22.	library	The library has some new books.	library
23.	tense	Use the past tense of go in a sentence.	tense
24.	gymnasium	Let's play basketball in the gymnasium.	gymnasium
25.	picturesque	The valley is very picturesque.	picturesque
26.	curiously	The cat sniffed curiously at the ball.	curiously
27.	steadily	Helen worked steadily into the night.	steadily
28.	microscope	Tracy focused the microscope carefully.	microscope
29.	modifier	An adjective is a modifier.	modifier
30.	eliminate	Eliminate the soft tomatoes from the basket.	eliminate
31.	substitute	Gary is a substitute bowler.	substitute
32.	interpret	Mark can interpret blueprints.	interpret
33.	extravagant	My brother bought his wife an extravagant gift.	extravagant
34.	silently	The boat moved silently through the water.	silently
35.	mysteriously	The key had mysteriously disappeared.	mysteriously
36.	dreadfully	The Smiths were dreadfully poor.	dreadfully
37.	ambitious	Caesar was ambitious.	ambitious
38.	contemptuously	Will contemptuously refused Don's help.	

contemptuously
LIFEPAC TEST cont...

39.	guilty	A person is innocent until proven guilty.	guilty
40.	thirsty	Jeff was very thirsty after the game.	thirsty
41.	wrathfully	Tom shouted wrathfully to Jim.	wrathfully
42.	decidedly	Her hair was decidedly red.	decidedly
43.	reliable	Joe is very reliable.	reliable
44.	wealthy	Danny is rather wealthy.	wealthy
45.	precious	A child is precious to his parents.	precious
46.	healthy	Eat well to stay healthy.	healthy
47.	timidly	Lisa walked in timidly.	timidly
48.	restlessly	Jimmy sat restlessly awaiting his turn.	restlessly
49.	quickly	Pete quickly threw the ball to first base.	quickly

ALTERNATE LIFEPAC TEST

1.	Sanskrit	The ancient writing must have been Sanskrit.	Sanskrit
2.	Indo-European	The Indo-European family includes French, English, and Irish.	Indo-European
3.	Semitic	Hebrew is a Semitic language.	Semitic
4.	Slavic	I don't know anyone who speaks Slavic.	Slavic
5.	peninsula	Florida is a peninsula.	peninsula
6.	dominion	Man has dominion over the animals.	dominion
7.	correlation	There is a direct correlation between studying and grades.	correlation
8.	comprise	Forty-eight states comprise the continental U.S.A.	comprise
9.	determiners	Determiners indicate nouns.	determiners
10.	noisily	The train rushed by noisily.	noisily
11.	starvation	Many people face starvation.	starvation
12.	specific	I gave Margie specific directions to my house.	specific
13.	sheepish	Roger has a sheepish expression.	sheepish
14.	insanely	Claude was insanely jealous.	insanely
15.	mansion	The old mansion was purchased for a hotel.	mansion
16.	rough	The golf ball was hit into the rough.	rough
17.	spattered	Rain spattered against the window panes.	spattered
18.	suddenly	Suddenly the sun broke through the clouds.	suddenly
19.	unpleasant	That was an unpleasant experience.	unpleasant
20.	reckless	George is a reckless driver.	reckless
21.	proudly	Tammy's mother proudly stood up.	proudly
22.	nervously	Lee nervously paced the floor.	nervously
23.	indignantly	The suspect indignantly denied the charge.	indignantly
24.	bitterly	Mrs. Gregg bitterly accused Terry of destroying her flowers.	bitterly
25.	clumsily	Ken clumsily walked across the floor.	clumsily
26.	dazzling	The jewelry was dazzling.	dazzling
27.	fascinating	Dolly Madison was a fascinating hostess.	fascinating
28.	fearfully	Kim fearfully proceeded down the dark hall.	fearfully
29.	timidly	Robert knocked timidly on the principal's door.	timidly
30.	silently	Joyce crept silently into bed.	silently
31.	mysterious	The mysterious stranger left quickly.	mysterious
32.	healthy	The cat appeared clean and healthy.	healthy

ALTERNATE LIFEPAC TEST cont...

33.	library	Carol is going to the town's <u>library</u> tomorrow.	<u>library</u>
34.	curiously	Timmy looked at the package <u>curiously</u>.	<u>curiously</u>
35.	gymnasium	Doug worked out in the <u>gymnasium</u>.	<u>gymnasium</u>
36.	microscope	Look at the slide under the <u>microscope</u>.	<u>microscope</u>
37.	communication	The telephone is a useful method of <u>communication</u>.	<u>communication</u>
38.	expression	What is the French <u>expression</u> for good-bye?	<u>expression</u>
39.	identify	Fingerprints are used to <u>identify</u> criminals.	<u>identify</u>
40.	separate	We would like <u>separate</u> checks for dinner.	<u>separate</u>
41.	symbol	The star of Bethlehem was a <u>symbol</u> of Christ's birth.	<u>symbol</u>
42.	signal	The <u>signal</u> at the railroad is broken.	<u>signal</u>
43.	eliminate	<u>Eliminate</u> desserts to lose weight.	<u>eliminate</u>
44.	picturesque	The Smoky Mountains are so <u>picturesque</u>.	<u>picturesque</u>
45.	bicycle	My <u>bicycle</u> has a flat tire.	<u>bicycle</u>
46.	ambitious	Carrie is a very <u>ambitious</u> person.	<u>ambitious</u>
47.	thirsty	Drink water when you are <u>thirsty</u>.	<u>thirsty</u>
48.	precious	A good name is more <u>precious</u> than riches.	<u>precious</u>
49.	guilty	Albert is <u>guilty</u> of cheating.	<u>guilty</u>

LIFEPAC TEST

1.	reliant	We are reliant upon our newsboy for daily papers.	reliant
2.	imminent	There was concern about the imminent return of the governor.	imminent
3.	elegant	Nancy wore an elegant gown at the recital.	elegant
4.	pulverize	The new juicer will pulverize the fruit.	pulverize
5.	surmise	It was easy to surmise what went wrong.	surmise
6.	edible	Our guide told us about the edible seeds.	edible
7.	amiable	The girl had an amiable personality.	amiable
8.	revise	A storm caused us to revise our travel plans.	revise
9.	vitalize	Eating the right food can vitalize your life.	vitalize
10.	unstable	The weather forecaster mentioned a mass of unstable conditions.	unstable
11.	profitable	Our community project proved to be profitable almost overnight.	profitable
12.	incredible	Advertisements boasted about the stuntman's incredible feat.	incredible
13.	itemize	Mother liked to itemize her grocery list.	itemize
14.	analyze	Take time to analyze your relationship with Christ.	analyze
15.	divisible	The number fifty is evenly divisible by ten.	divisible
16.	probable	Their doctor diagnosed the probable cause of the illness.	probable
17.	supervise	Judy was chosen to supervise the summer program.	supervise
18.	sterilize	Our class learned how to sterilize bandages.	sterilize
19.	intolerant	They discovered some of the primitive tribes were intolerant of outsiders.	intolerant
20.	energize	A battery charger is used to energize old batteries.	energize
21.	advertise	Sales will increase if we advertise our product.	advertise
22.	realize	The diver did not realize how deep the lake was.	realize
23.	attachable	His radio was attachable to his bicycle.	attachable
24.	supplement	Some people supplement their diet with vitamins.	supplement
25.	indifferent	One student had an indifferent attitude toward his science class.	indifferent

LIFEPAC TEST cont...

26.	petulant	He was bothered by his uncle's petulant nature.	petulant
27.	transplant	Help was needed to transplant all the trees.	transplant
28.	eminent	Several eminent physicians were called in on the case.	eminent
29.	pressurize	Twenty pounds of air was needed to pressurize the tire.	pressurize
30.	lovable	She was surprised by her lovable new pet.	lovable
31.	sensible	Father always gives us sensible advice.	sensible
32.	eligible	Only the eligible voters were given the ballots.	eligible
33.	collapsible	Peter shopped for a collapsible chair.	collapsible
34.	patronize	People patronize restaurants with good food.	patronize
35.	polarize	The campaign speeches tended to polarize the candidate.	polarize
36.	paralyze	Polio can still paralyze people who do not take the vaccine.	paralyze
37.	covenant	A covenant is a binding agreement.	covenant
38.	variant	They could find only one spelling variant in the words.	variant
39.	exercise	To feel better, you should exercise regularly.	exercise
40.	dehumanize	Using numbers instead of names for identification can dehumanize people.	dehumanize
41.	characterize	You could characterize him as being conservative.	characterize
42.	confident	The team's coach was more confident than anyone.	confident
43.	significant	Most of the ideas were significant.	significant
44.	impudent	The impudent child kept interrupting.	impudent
45.	utilize	Plans were made to utilize the entire building.	utilize
46.	compromise	Aunt Ruth would never compromise a principle.	compromise
47.	idolize	A three-year old youngster can idolize all kinds of objects.	idolize
48.	defensible	John's argument would have been defensible last week.	defensible
49.	excusable	Her absence was excusable by the principal.	excusable
50.	despicable	The neighbors were upset over the despicable crime.	despicable

ALTERNATE LIFEPAC TEST

1. reliable — We sent the clock to a reliable repairman. — reliable
2. infallible — Human beings are not infallible. — infallible
3. noticeable — The man had a noticeable limp. — noticeable
4. responsible — We are responsible to God for our actions. — responsible
5. hesitant — The patient was hesitant about eating lunch. — hesitant
6. pertinent — List only the pertinent facts. — pertinent
7. complement — The frame seemed to complement the picture. — complement
8. remise — He was forced to remise his land. — remise
9. mesmerize — Andy pretended to mesmerize the dog. — mesmerize
10. galvanize — An early defeat served to galvanize the team effort. — galvanize
11. recreant — Fellow soldiers could not understand the corporal's recreant act. — recreant
12. vigilant — The police dog maintained a vigilant watch. — vigilant
13. elegant — Critics said the party was too elegant for the town. — elegant
14. itemize — His pen went dry before he could itemize all the mistakes. — itemize
15. surmise — Investigators arrived to surmise the situation. — surmise
16. exercise — Betty was told to exercise her dog every day. — exercise
17. characterize — It was difficult to characterize the new city hall. — characterize
18. eminent — Eminent scholars were able to understand the ancient writings. — eminent
19. durable — Metal pails appeared to be more durable than plastics. — durable
20. excusable — His unusual actions were not excusable. — excusable
21. supervise — The older children tried to supervise the younger ones. — supervise
22. polarize — They needed filters that would polarize the light. — polarize
23. subservient — In the Middle Ages peasants were subservient to the lord of the manor. — subservient
24. imminent — Authorities said there was no imminent danger. — imminent
25. probable — No probable cause of the injury was listed. — probable

ALTERNATE LIFEPAC TEST cont...

26. profitable   The ice cream route was not very   profitable
                   profitable in the winter.
27. reprehensive   Nothing could be more reprehensive   reprehensive
                   than the crime that was committed.
28. lovable   All babies are lovable.   lovable
29. edible   We grew only edible fruit on our farm.   edible
30. despicable   Fortunately, there was only one despicable   despicable
                   character in the book.
31. unstable   Use of rocks made an unstable walkway.   unstable
32. transplant   A kidney transplant was necessary.   transplant
33. reliant   The reliant young man got the job.   reliant
34. defensible   Without armament, the surrounded city   defensible
                   was not defensible.
35. accessible   Our lake cabin was accessible only by boat.   accessible
36. resilient   How resilient is the tennis ball?   resilient
37. electrolyze   Caution was taken in the project to   electrolyze
                   electrolyze the chemicals.
38. somnolent   Babies usually become somnolent after   somnolent
                   eating.
39. inevitable   Conflict between some nations seems   inevitable
                   inevitable.
40. permissible   It was not permissible to leave the   permissible
                   classroom.
41. recalcitrant   The farmer was anxious to get rid of   recalcitrant
                   the recalcitrant mule.
42. significant   Nothing significant was broadcast on   significant
                   the news program.
43. confident   You can be confident about your salvation   confident
                   in Christ.
44. unmatchable   The socks were unmatchable because of   unmatchable
                   their different colors.

LIFEPAC TEST

1. abbreviation   AZ is an abbreviation for Arizona.   abbreviation
2. aisle   The bride walked down the aisle.   aisle
3. arid   Phoenix has an arid climate.   arid
4. congenial   Sarah has a congenial personality.   congenial
5. dexterous   The dexterous artist painted a scene of   dexterous
                   the Grand Canyon.
6. docile   The docile child followed her father   docile
                   home.
7. homonym   Pear is a homonym of pare.   homonym
8. infinite   God has infinite wisdom.   infinite
9. orient   He had to orient himself to the new   orient
                   teacher.
10. psalmist   The psalmist wrote songs to God.   psalmist
11. sluggard   The man was a sluggard and refused   sluggard
                   to work.
12. synonym   Sleepy is a synonym of tired.   synonym
13. undaunted   The undaunted fireman rescued her from   undaunted
                   the blazing house.
14. unyielding   The Christian was unyielding in the   unyielding
                   face of persecution.
15. obedient   Mary, an obedient child, did as her   obedient
                   father asked.
16. saturation   The sponge had not yet reached the point   saturation
                   of saturation.
17. envelope   Tom put a stamp on the envelope.   envelope
18. handicap   The lack of a player did not handicap   handicap
                   the team.
19. dictionary   A dictionary contains meanings of words.   dictionary
20. macron   A macron shows that a vowel should   macron
                   have a long sound.
21. diacritical   Diacritical marks were placed over the   diacritical
                   letters to show their pronunciation.
22. aviation   The Wright brothers began modern day   aviation
                   aviation.
23. pronunciation Words should be said with correct   pronunciation
                   pronunciation.
24. bouquet   George sent a bouquet of daisies   bouquet
                   to his girlfriend.
25. horrid   The horrid plane crash caused many   horrid
                   deaths.
26. international   International intervention failed to bring   international
                   peace in Vietnam.

LIFEPAC TEST cont...

27.	personal	The information in the letter was personal.	personal
28.	honesty	Honesty is the best policy.	honesty
29.	zoology	Zoology is the study of animal life.	zoology
30.	ceiling	The ceiling leaked when it rained.	ceiling
31.	merciful	The merciful king spared his life.	merciful
32.	separate	Miss Olsen had to separate the talking students.	separate
33.	commentator	The news commentator told about the President's election.	commentator
34.	semester	James did well in his first semester of school.	semester
35.	opaque	An inch of dust made the window opaque.	opaque
36.	yeast	Yeast makes bread rise.	yeast
37.	believe	I believe in miracles.	believe
38.	Italian	The Italian peninsula is shaped like a boot.	Italian
39.	friendliness	The friendliness of the congregation attracted me to the church.	friendliness
40.	Arkansas	Arkansas has a small population.	Arkansas
41.	diligence	It takes diligence to get through school.	diligence
42.	rebirth	The Christian has experienced rebirth.	rebirth
43.	alcoholic	The hospital has a special ward for alcoholic patients.	alcoholic
44.	altogether	Charlie's answer was altogether incorrect.	altogether
45.	vitality	Her life was filled with a vitality not common in many people.	vitality
46.	serenity	Grandmother was filled with a quiet serenity.	serenity
47.	tranquility	The tranquility in her life was made possible by Christ.	tranquility
48.	purity	The purity of Jesus is beyond question.	purity
49.	humility	The humility of Paul is an example for all Christians.	humility
50.	spirituality	John is well known for his spirituality.	spirituality

ALTERNATE LIFEPAC TEST

1.	accommodate	The schoolroom was not large enough to accommodate seventy students.	accommodate
2.	antonym	Love is an antonym of hate.	antonym
3.	communication	The telegraph is an early form of communication.	communication
4.	deceit	The angelic boy did not look capable of deceit.	deceit
5.	dexterous	The dexterous artist painted a scene of the Grand Canyon.	dexterous
6.	holy	". . . The temple of God is holy, which temple ye are." (1 Corinthians 3:17)	holy
7.	infiltrated	The enemy soldier infiltrated their lines of defense.	infiltrated
8.	isle	They were shipwrecked on a Pacific isle.	isle
9.	orient	He had to orient himself to the new teacher.	orient
10.	psalmist	The psalmist wrote songs to God.	psalmist
11.	slothful	The slothful child would not clean his room.	slothful
12.	synonym	Sleepy is a synonym of tired.	synonym
13.	thesaurus	I looked for a synonym for the word blend in the thesaurus.	thesaurus
14.	undaunted	The undaunted fireman rescued her from the blazing house.	undaunted
15.	unity	The unity of the thirteen colonies made them a stronger nation.	unity
16.	wholly	Paul understood wholly the words of his mother.	wholly
17.	salvation	If you accept Jesus Christ as Saviour, you obtain eternal salvation.	salvation
18.	saturation	The sponge had not yet reached the point of saturation.	saturation
19.	conservation	Conservation of the worlds resources is vital.	conservation
20.	envelope	Tom put a stamp on the envelope.	envelope
21.	accent	Helga spoke with a German accent.	accent
22.	forehead	Jane bumped her forehead on the car.	forehead
23.	advertisement	In order to sell his car George placed an advertisement in the newspaper.	advertisement
24.	vocabulary	Sandy studied the vocabulary words.	vocabulary
25.	personnel	Rick was the head of personnel for his company.	personnel

ALTERNATE LIFEPAC TEST cont...

26.	breve	A breve shows that a vowel has a short sound.	breve
27.	pronounce	Jim could not pronounce the word.	pronounce
28.	rebellion	The rebellion of the colonists was successful.	rebellion
29.	international	International intervention failed to bring peace in Vietnam.	international
30.	director	Randy is the director of recreation at the park.	director
31.	forfeit	Debbie's softball team had to forfeit the game.	forfeit
32.	biology	Evelyn wanted to study biology in college.	biology
33.	seize	The teacher had to seize the arms of the struggling boy.	seize
34.	merciful	The merciful king spared his life.	merciful
35.	temperance	We should employ temperance in our behavior.	temperance
36.	humorous	Sandy is a humorous person.	humorous
37.	contraction	Swimming cramps are caused by the contraction of muscles.	contraction
38.	slang	Slang expressions should not be used in writing.	slang
39.	yeast	Yeast makes bread rise.	yeast
40.	benefit	Richard's skill would benefit the class.	benefit
41.	compassion	Christ had compassion upon us sinners.	compassion
42.	anything	You can have anything you want.	anything
43.	apostle	Paul was an apostle of Christ.	apostle
44.	aggravate	He can really aggravate me!	aggravate
45.	accidental	The breaking of the window was accidental.	accidental
46.	all right	Mom, is it all right if I play with Johnny?	all right
47.	vitality	Her life was filled with a vitality not common in many people.	vitality
48.	responsibility	It is your responsibility to obey your parents.	responsibility
49.	maturity	As Laura grew older, she gained in maturity.	maturity
50.	humility	The humility of Paul is an example to Christians.	humility

LIFEPAC TEST

1.	principal	Mr. Stone is the principal of Grandview Elementary School.	principal
2.	principle	The resurrection of Jesus Christ is a principle of Christian faith.	principle
3.	all ready	Everything is all ready to go.	all ready
4.	whether	He asked the student whether they wanted to go or stay.	whether
5.	temerity	What temerity he had to ask such a question.	temerity
6.	implicit	We have implicit confidence in our teacher.	implicit
7.	compliment	The teacher gave his student a compliment.	compliment
8.	complement	This book will complement his library.	complement
9.	convex	Convex lenses are curved out.	convex
10.	condone	The judge could not condone the criminal action.	condone
11.	illegible	The letter was illegible.	illegible
12.	former	The former president of the company came to town.	former
13.	effect	The thunderstorm made a terrible effect on the city.	effect
14.	counsel	She went to the pastor for his counsel in the matter.	counsel
15.	altogether	Altogether there were 40 students in the classroom.	altogether
16.	except	Except for Matthew, everyone went to the park.	except
17.	accept	I will accept his offer to work at the store.	accept
18.	feign	To feign means to pretend.	feign
19.	faint	He has a faint voice.	faint
20.	incidental	It was incidental that the two men met on the street corner.	incidental
21.	abbreviation	The abbreviation for the word mister is capital "Mr."	abbreviation
22.	quotation marks	Quotation marks need to be placed around a direct quote.	quotation marks
23.	inclusive	Be sure you have made an inclusive list of items for the trip.	inclusive
24.	preference	His preference is for cake rather than ice cream.	preference
25.	capitalization	Susan forgot the rules of capitalization.	capitalization

LIFEPAC TEST cont...

26.	restaurant	The restaurant serves delicious food.	restaurant
27.	down-in-the-mouth	He was down-in-the-mouth because he lost the race.	down in the-mouth
28.	objective	The objective is to hit the ball.	objective
29.	hyphen	The hyphen is a mark used to join parts of a compound word.	hyphen
30.	suffix	The suffix "-ed" is used to form the past tense of many verbs.	suffix
31.	possessive	Tom is very possessive of his new bicycle.	possessive
32.	contraction	A contraction can be made from the words can and not.	contraction
33.	cradle-to-grave	The expression cradle-to-grave can be used in place of the word "lifetime."	cradle-to-grave
34.	parentheses	Parentheses are often used in mathematics.	parentheses
35.	pre-existent	The word pre-existent is used to describe Jesus Christ.	pre-existent
36.	quoted	Tom was quoted in the newspaper story in regards to the baseball game.	quoted
37.	president-elect	President-elect Mike Thomas will not take over the control of the student council until November.	president-elect

ALTERNATE LIFEPAC TEST

1.	principal	Mr. Stone is the principal of Grandview Elementary School.	principal
2.	already	The new books have already arrived.	already
3.	weather	There is supposed to be good weather for the game today.	weather
4.	timidity	God has not given us the spirit of timidity.	timidity
5.	explicit	The directions were very explicit.	explicit
6.	complement	This book will complement his library.	complement
7.	concave	This glass is concave.	concave
8.	condemn	I do not condemn you for what you did.	condemn
9.	eligible	He is eligible for a pay raise.	eligible
10.	illegible	The letter was illegible.	illegible
11.	formal	He has a formal manner when he speaks to businessmen.	formal
12.	affect	Did the new price increase affect your father's business?	affect
13.	council	The city council will vote on the new resolution tomorrow.	council
14.	all together	They went to the zoo all together.	all together
15.	except	Except for Matthew, everyone went to the park.	except
16.	accept	I will accept his offer to work at the store.	accept
17.	faint	He has a faint voice.	faint
18.	ultra-articulate	The speaker was ultra-articulate.	ultra-articulate
19.	abbreviation	The abbreviation for the word mister is capital "Mr."	abbreviation
20.	syllable	The word "strong" has only one syllable.	syllable
21.	inclusive	Be sure you have made an inclusive list of items for the trip.	inclusive
22.	italics	These letters are printed in italics.	italics
23.	capitalization	Susan forgot the rules of capitalization.	capitalization
24.	restaurant	The restaurant serves delicious food.	restaurant
25.	apostrophe	The apostrophe is used to show possession.	apostrophe
26.	plural	The plural of girl is girls.	plural
27.	prefix	The prefix "ultra" means excessive or extreme.	prefix
28.	dialectal	Dialectal is a word used as an adjective.	dialectal
29.	possessive	Tom is very possessive of his new bicycle.	possessive
30.	miscellaneous	Mark has a miscellaneous collection of stamps.	miscellaneous
31.	singular	The word "man" is a singular noun.	singular

ALTERNATE LIFEPAC TEST cont...

32.	cradle-to-grave	The expression cradle-to-grave can be used in place of the word "lifetime."	cradle-to-grave
33.	semi-independent	The company is not considered to be independent but semi-independent.	semi-independent
34.	parentheses	Parentheses are often used in mathematics.	parentheses
35.	self-satisfaction	He did the job for his own self-satisfaction.	self-satisfaction
36.	pre-existent	The word pre-existent is used to describe Jesus Christ.	pre-existent
37.	ridiculous	Mary told her friends a ridiculous and humorous story.	ridiculous

LIFEPAC TEST

1.	intelligence	She has a lot of intelligence.	intelligence
2.	remembrance	The act of remembering is remembrance.	remembrance
3.	alliance	Our country made an alliance with West Germany.	alliance
4.	repentance	The act of repenting a sin is called repentance.	repentance
5.	vigilance	Keep a watchful vigilance for the thieves.	vigilance
6.	condolence	Let me offer my condolence to you.	condolence
7.	condense	To condense means to shorten.	condense
8.	intense	He had an intense look on his face.	intense
9.	nonsense	That story was full of nonsense.	nonsense
10.	existence	It is easy to prove God's existence.	existence
11.	perseverance	We must have perseverance.	perseverance
12.	immense	That rock must be immense.	immense
13.	interference	We will not allow any interference.	interference
14.	superintendence	Guidance and direction are two words that describe superintendence.	superintendence
15.	amiable	She is an amiable person.	amiable
16.	barbarous	They are a barbarous people.	barbarous
17.	burglary	He was convicted of burglary.	burglary
18.	disastrous	There was a disastrous flood that hit our town yesterday.	disastrous
19.	formerly	He was formerly associated with that company.	formerly
20.	government	Our government tries to help as much as possible.	government
21.	irrelevant	His argument was irrelevant.	irrelevant
22.	lightning	The lightning struck the telephone pole.	lightning
23.	laboratory	He conducts many experiments in the laboratory.	laboratory
24.	mischievous	We have a mischievous dog.	mischievous
25.	perform	The band will perform at half time.	perform
26.	probably	We will probably go to the park tomorrow.	probably
27.	tragedy	We saw a Greek tragedy, or play.	tragedy
28.	sacrilegious	What he did was considered sacrilegious.	sacrilegious
29.	suffrage	The right to vote is called suffrage.	suffrage
30.	undoubtedly	He will undoubtedly win the race.	undoubtedly
31.	narrative	He wrote a descriptive story and a narrative one.	narrative
32.	elongated	The piece of wood was elongated at one end.	elongated

LIFEPAC TEST cont...

33.	scrupulous	He is a scrupulous individual.	scrupulous
34.	census	A census is taken every ten years.	census
35.	precipitous	The cliff was very precipitous.	precipitous
36.	conical	The drawing had a conical shape to it.	conical
37.	reluctantly	Susan reluctantly went to the store.	reluctantly
38.	galvanized	The metal was not galvanized.	galvanized
39.	maligned	She was maligned and mistreated.	maligned
40.	profusion	There was a profusion of food available.	profusion
41.	eminence	Eminence means to have a rank or position above all or most others.	eminence
42.	fallibility	Everyone has some fallibility.	fallibility
43.	controversies	There were many controversies over the situation.	controversies
44.	vaguely	She vaguely remembers the incident.	vaguely
45.	rural	She lives in a rural area.	rural

ALTERNATE LIFEPAC TEST

1.	acceptance	We all want to have acceptance in some group.	acceptance
2.	intelligence	She has a lot of intelligence.	intelligence
3.	remembrance	The act of remembering is remembrance.	remembrance
4.	defense	That team has a good defense.	defense
5.	repentance	The act of repenting a sin is called repentance.	repentance
6.	alliance	Our country made an alliance with West Germany.	alliance
7.	attendance	There was a big attendance at the concert.	attendance
8.	expense	Spare no expense in the preparation.	expense
9.	condense	To condense means to shorten.	condense
10.	intense	He had an intense look on his face.	intense
11.	resemblance	She has a remarkable resemblance to my sister.	resemblance
12.	conference	The leaders of the town held a conference.	conference
13.	experience	She had a pleasant experience.	experience
14.	perseverance	We must have perseverance.	perseverance
15.	resistance	How much resistance does that metal have to rust?	resistance
16.	grievance	What grievance has he caused you?	grievance
17.	occurrence	The occurrence took place on Saturday.	occurrence
18.	vengeance	Vengeance belongs to the Lord.	vengeance
19.	athletic	He is very athletic.	athletic
20.	brethren	Brethren in the New Testament refers to the fellow members of a church or group.	brethren
21.	formally	We were formally invited to a party.	formally
22.	government	Our government tries to help as much as possible.	government
23.	irreverent	How could you be so irreverent?	irreverent
24.	lightning	The lightning struck the telephone pole.	lightning
25.	laboratory	He conducts many experiments in the laboratory.	laboratory
26.	mathematician	He is a great mathematician.	mathematician
27.	momentous	What a momentous occasion.	momentous
28.	prerogative	The government has the prerogative to tax us.	prerogative
29.	tentative	The tentative date for the party is tomorrow.	tentative
30.	sacrilegious	What he did was considered sacrilegious.	sacrilegious
31.	surprise	He had a surprise waiting for his Dad.	surprise

ALTERNATE LIFEPAC TEST cont...

32.	narrative	He wrote a descriptive story and a narrative one.	narrative
33.	irrelevant	What he said was irrelevant to the defense.	irrelevant
34.	elongated	The piece of wood was elongated at one end.	elongated
35.	subsistence	They were living on a limited subsistence.	subsistence
36.	census	A census is taken every ten years.	census
37.	visage	His visage or fare had changed.	visage
38.	consternation	There is no need for consternation.	consternation
39.	reluctantly	Susan reluctantly went to the store.	reluctantly
40.	prominent	Bill is a prominent businessman.	prominent
41.	oscillations	The machine produced many oscillations.	oscillations
42.	sedulously	They sedulously put the house together.	sedulously
43.	fallibility	Everyone has some fallibility.	fallibility
44.	cistern	They held the water in the cistern.	cistern
45.	rural	She lived in a rural area.	rural

LIFEPAC TEST

1. <u>acquire</u>   The school will <u>acquire</u> new books this fall.   <u>acquire</u>
2. <u>solemn</u>   The <u>solemn</u> look on Nancy's face made everyone aware that a problem had arisen.   <u>solemn</u>
3. <u>indebtedness</u>   How can I ever repay my <u>indebtedness</u> to you?   <u>indebtedness</u>
4. <u>succumb</u>   Do not <u>succumb</u> to temptation.   <u>succumb</u>
5. <u>condemn</u>   You do not have the right to <u>condemn</u> someone for their actions.   <u>condemn</u>
6. <u>writhe</u>   After being called on, Kathy began to <u>writhe</u> uncomfortably in her seat.   <u>writhe</u>
7. <u>guarantee</u>   The company will <u>guarantee</u> the product.   <u>guarantee</u>
8. <u>scissors</u>   Will you please pass the <u>scissors</u> to me?   <u>scissors</u>
9. <u>colonel</u>   The <u>colonel</u> will retire from the army next May.   <u>colonel</u>
10. <u>acknowledge</u>   Please <u>acknowledge</u> all the books used in your report.   <u>acknowledge</u>
11. <u>annihilate</u>   The entomologist is going to <u>annihilate</u> the termite colony.   <u>annihilate</u>
12. <u>pneumonia</u>   When I was small, I had a bad case of <u>pneumonia</u>.   <u>pneumonia</u>
13. <u>adjourned</u>   The court was <u>adjourned</u> until nine o'clock Wednesday morning.   <u>adjourned</u>
14. <u>auxiliary</u>   The ladies' <u>auxiliary</u> will prepare the banquet.   <u>auxiliary</u>
15. <u>circuit</u>   The <u>circuit</u> judge will arrive in two weeks.   <u>circuit</u>
16. <u>exhausted</u>   The puppy was <u>exhausted</u> after playing with his toys.   <u>exhausted</u>
17. <u>exhilarate</u>   The teacher will <u>exhilarate</u> her class by taking them on a field trip.   <u>exhilarate</u>
18. <u>lieutenant</u>   Michael was a <u>lieutenant</u> in the service.   <u>lieutenant</u>
19. <u>parliament</u>   The British <u>parliament</u> will meet to discuss the proposed law.   <u>parliament</u>
20. <u>receipt</u>   Please retain your sales <u>receipt</u> if you wish to return an item.   <u>receipt</u>
21. <u>rheumatism</u>   Many people in the world suffer from <u>rheumatism</u>.   <u>rheumatism</u>
22. <u>shepherd</u>   The <u>shepherd</u> watched over his flock.   <u>shepherd</u>
23. <u>stretched</u>   Billy <u>stretched</u> a muscle in the last race.   <u>stretched</u>
24. <u>vehicle</u>   The radio is used as <u>vehicle</u> to carry God's message to many people.   <u>vehicle</u>
25. <u>tongue</u>   The <u>tongue</u> of my shoe is ripped.   <u>tongue</u>

LIFEPAC TEST cont...

26.	advertisement	The advertisement placed in the paper gave tremendous results.	advertisement
27.	analysis	The analysis of the blood sample proved negative.	analysis
28.	benefited	The cut in taxes benefited many citizens.	benefited
29.	coma	A prayer request was made for Liza to regain consciousness from a coma.	coma
30.	competition	The competition for the scholarship was difficult.	competition
31.	corps	The corps of nurses and missionaries will leave for Senegal in March.	corps
32.	desirable	It is most desirable to carry auto insurance.	desirable
33.	existence	The existence of dinosaurs has been proven.	existence
34.	forty	We picked forty bushels of apples from our orchard.	forty
35.	guard	Be on your guard for storm clouds today.	guard
36.	maintenance	The maintenance of our church is a large responsibility.	maintenance
37.	opportunity	Take every opportunity you have to further your education.	opportunity
38.	repetition	There was an unusual amount of repetition in his speech.	repetition
39.	separate	Please separate your report into three sections.	separate
40.	tormentor	He was a tormentor of the early Christians.	tormentor

ALTERNATE LIFEPAC TEST

1.	wholly	Our church has committed itself wholly to the missionary project.	wholly
2.	psychology	My new psychology class meets at 9:35 a.m. on Tuesday.	psychology
3.	indebtedness	How can I ever repay my indebtedness to you?	indebtedness
4.	acquaint	Please acquaint yourselves with the new attendance system.	acquaint
5.	subtle	The salesman was very subtle with his words.	subtle
6.	mortgage	For the first time in our lives, we do not have to pay a mortgage.	mortgage
7.	indict	The grand jury will indict the accused sometime this week.	indict
8.	circuit	The circuit was broken causing the lights to go out.	circuit
9.	asthma	Children and adults alike suffer from asthma.	asthma
10.	abridge	We plan to abridge our first edition.	abridge
11.	acknowledge	Please acknowledge all the books used in your report.	acknowledge
12.	poignant	Skunks spray a very poignant odor when provoked.	poignant
13.	adjourned	The court was adjourned until nine o'clock Wednesday morning.	adjourned
14.	aisle	Suzie was the happiest girl in the world as she walked down the aisle on her wedding day.	aisle
15.	arctic	The arctic climate is very cold.	arctic
16.	bouquet	The spring bouquet I received was very beautiful.	bouquet
17.	eighth	Johnny is in the eighth grade at school.	eighth
18.	height	The monsoon season is at its height in August.	height
19.	isthmus	A canal was constructed across the isthmus.	isthmus
20.	lieutenant	Michael was a lieutenant in the service.	lieutenant
21.	pageant	The children's Christmas pageant was truly delightful.	pageant
22.	rhyme	When composing your poems, try to make the lines rhyme.	rhyme
23.	sovereignty	The king showed his sovereignty by force.	sovereignty

ALTERNATE LIFEPAC TEST cont...

24.	thoroughly	Go over your figures <u>thoroughly</u> before handing in your papers.	thoroughly
25.	twelfth	This is my <u>twelfth</u> year with the company.	twelfth
26.	virtue	A good <u>virtue</u> is caring for your fellow man.	virtue
27.	adequate	I hope we have <u>adequate</u> water stored for the summer.	adequate
28.	advertisement	The <u>advertisement</u> placed in the paper gave tremendous results.	advertisement
29.	bachelor	Hank was a <u>bachelor</u> until he was 30 years of age.	bachelor
30.	calendar	A skating party is on the church <u>calendar</u> for this month.	calendar
31.	comparative	The use of <u>comparative</u> statements helps a person better understand what he is reading.	comparative
32.	complement	The entire ship's <u>complement</u> was at hand for the festivities.	complement
33.	description	The witness was called upon to give a <u>description</u> of the assailant.	description
34.	dissipate	The clouds began to <u>dissipate</u>.	dissipate
35.	February	Our Sunday school class is going skiing in <u>February</u>.	February
36.	imperative	It is <u>imperative</u> that I see the commander.	imperative
37.	maintenance	The <u>maintenance</u> of our church is a large responsibility.	maintenance
38.	minutes	We must leave for the plane in twenty <u>minutes</u>.	minutes
39.	repetition	There was an unusual amount of <u>repetition</u> in his speech.	repetition
40.	whether	<u>Whether</u> or not we go on the picnic will depend upon father's work.	whether

LIFEPAC TEST

1. <u>adversary</u> — The sandstorm proved an admirable <u>adversary</u>. — <u>adversary</u>
2. <u>arrangement</u> — The floral <u>arrangement</u> consisted of carnations and babies' breath. — <u>arrangement</u>
3. <u>asterisk</u> — The <u>asterisk</u> at the bottom of the page gives more information. — <u>asterisk</u>
4. <u>bizarre</u> — A snowstorm in southern Arizona is truly <u>bizarre</u>. — <u>bizarre</u>
5. <u>comparatively</u> — Gasoline prices are <u>comparatively</u> higher than last week. — <u>comparatively</u>
6. <u>conscience</u> — My <u>conscience</u> bothered me after I accidentally broke the dish. — <u>conscience</u>
7. <u>convenience</u> — It is such a <u>convenience</u> having a helpful family. — <u>convenience</u>
8. <u>courageous</u> — The <u>courageous</u> ski patrol searched for the lost boy in a blinding snowstorm. — <u>courageous</u>
9. <u>definitely</u> — The hockey game will <u>definitely</u> be played on Thursday. — <u>definitely</u>
10. <u>disguise</u> — We had a great time at the <u>disguise</u> party. — <u>disguise</u>
11. <u>existence</u> — We owe our very <u>existence</u> to God. — <u>existence</u>
12. <u>forty-five</u> — The plane will be leaving in <u>forty-five</u> minutes. — <u>forty-five</u>
13. <u>gasoline</u> — We ran out of <u>gasoline</u> in the middle of the lake. — <u>gasoline</u>
14. <u>interest</u> — The idea of singing for the church is of great <u>interest</u> to me. — <u>interest</u>
15. <u>library</u> — The <u>library</u> can be a great source of information. — <u>library</u>
16. <u>nomination</u> — The <u>nomination</u> was seconded and carried by the committee. — <u>nomination</u>
17. <u>relation</u> — The <u>relation</u> between poverty and disease can be seen worldwide. — <u>relation</u>
18. <u>shining</u> — The sun was <u>shining</u> through the rain clouds. — <u>shining</u>
19. <u>Wednesday</u> — Patti and I plan to leave on <u>Wednesday</u> morning. — <u>Wednesday</u>
20. <u>ascent</u> — Christ's <u>ascent</u> into Heaven must have been a beautiful sight. — <u>ascent</u>
21. <u>assent</u> — Dad gave his <u>assent</u> for us to go on the trip. — <u>assent</u>
22. <u>cent</u> — I do not have a <u>cent</u> to my name. — <u>cent</u>
23. <u>cord</u> — The <u>cord</u> held the rowboat to the dock during the storm. — <u>cord</u>

LIFEPAC TEST cont...

24.	I'll	I'll be with you in a moment.	I'll
25.	medal	Bob won a medal for his sportsmanship.	medal
26.	meddle	I prefer not to meddle in someone else's affairs.	meddle
27.	metal	The metal tent spikes are stronger than the plastic type.	metal
28.	sight	I have the cabin in sight.	sight
29.	site	The excavation site was in the middle of an orchard.	site
30.	their	Their team is ahead right now.	their
31.	they're	They're going to the mountains on vacation.	They're
32.	all right	The answers given were all right.	all right
33.	bicycle	Our Young Adults class is planning a bicycle trip.	bicycle
34.	dolphin	The dolphin jumped through the fire hoop at the end of the show.	dolphin
35.	eugenics	Hitler tried to improve the human race by the use of eugenics.	eugenics
36.	facial	The facial expression on the statue was very comical.	facial
37.	government	The government has lifted all controls on oil prices.	government
38.	hydraulic	The hydraulic jack was used to lift the car.	hydraulic
39.	intervene	The government may intervene if the strike continues.	intervene
40.	mother-in-law	Bob cannot go this evening because his mother-in-law is visiting.	mother-in-law
41.	occasional	An occasional shower may arise, but it is very rare.	occasional
42.	plaid	The Scottish kilt is a plaid skirt worn by the highlanders.	plaid
43.	restaurant	We went to a fantastic restaurant to celebrate my birthday.	restaurant
44.	therefore	Therefore, the proposed new freeway will take ten years to build.	therefore
45.	who's	Who's sponsoring the softball team this year?	who's

ALTERNATE LIFEPAC TEST

1. alien   Foreign languages are <u>alien</u> to most parents.   alien
2. assassin   John Wilkes Booth was an <u>assassin</u>.   assassin
3. beautiful   The peacock opened its tail to show a   beautiful
                   <u>beautiful</u> array of colors.
4. buried   The pirate <u>buried</u> his treasure on the   buried
                   sandy beach.
5. conference   The teachers <u>conference</u> was held in   conference
                   Topeka, Kansas.
6. consequential In the <u>consequential</u> debate the new   consequential
                   candidate will be chosen.
7. counterfeit   The man was questioned about the   counterfeit
                   <u>counterfeit</u> money in his possession.
8. handkerchief   Suzie bought her father a <u>handkerchief</u> for   handkerchief
                   his birthday.
9. pharmacy   The local <u>pharmacy</u> burned down last   pharmacy
                   night.
10. surprise   I was in total <u>surprise</u> when I won the   surprise
                   baking contest.
11. triumph   The race ended in <u>triumph</u> for the   triumph
                   youngster.
12. aisle   The church <u>aisle</u> was packed with visitors.   aisle
13. chord   The <u>chord</u> was held too long in that   chord
                   measure.
14. cite   A policeman will <u>cite</u> you for littering.   cite
15. isle   The <u>isle</u> was inhabited by a colony of   isle
                   chimps.
16. pore   Oil comes from a <u>pore</u> in your skin.   pore
17. pour   Please <u>pour</u> me a glass of lemonade.   pour
18. scent   The <u>scent</u> of the orange blossoms is very   scent
                   sweet.
19. sent   My parents <u>sent</u> me a bouquet of flowers   sent
                   for my birthday.
20. sew   I love to <u>sew</u> new clothes for summer.   sew
21. so   I have finished the laundry <u>so</u> we can   so
                   leave now.
22. sow   Father plans to <u>sow</u> the east pasture.   sow
23. to   I planned <u>to</u> go fishing in the White   to
                   Mountains.
24. too   There will be snow in the upper regions   too
                   <u>too</u>.
25. two   Please reserve <u>two</u> seats in my name.   two

ALTERNATE LIFEPAC TEST cont...

26.	vain	"Thou shalt not take the name of the Lord thy God in vain."	vain
27.	vein	The vein in the gold mine stretched for miles.	vein
28.	vane	The weather vane spun wildly during the storm.	vane
29.	attention	If you don't pay attention to the road signs, we may get lost.	attention
30.	calendar	The church calendar is full for the month of May.	calendar
31.	copies	We need twenty more copies for the choir.	copies
32.	despair	When you have a problem do not despair.	despair
33.	epitaph	If Christ had lived today, what would you write as His epitaph?	epitaph
34.	extraneous	The material contained many extraneous ideas.	extraneous
35.	gregarious	Sheep are gregarious in nature.	gregarious
36.	height	The Rocky Mountains have more height than the Appalachians.	height
37.	inhibition	I have an inhibition about speaking in public.	inhibition
38.	kidnapped	The kidnapped child was found unharmed.	kidnapped
39.	nausea	I usually experience nausea when I fly.	nausea
40.	occasionally	Occasionally we find a need for more help.	occasionally
41.	probably	The basketball game will probably go into overtime.	probably
42.	rhetoric	The rhetoric in Presidential campaigns is important.	rhetoric
43.	spoonfuls	The baby had two spoonfuls and upset the bowl.	spoonfuls
44.	twine	The twine broke and my kite came crashing to the ground.	twine
45.	existence	We owe our very existence to God.	existence

LIFEPAC TEST

1.	absence	Joseph's <u>absence</u> from the team was noticed by everyone.	absence
2.	accommodate	The school bus could not <u>accommodate</u> all the students.	accommodate
3.	acknowledge	Dr. Hill did not <u>acknowledge</u> my question.	acknowledge
4.	acquire	How did you <u>acquire</u> such a positive attitude?	acquire
5.	aggressive	My friend was extremely <u>aggressive</u> this morning.	aggressive
6.	anxious	The Bible tells us to trust the Lord and not be <u>anxious</u>.	anxious
7.	apparent	It was very <u>apparent</u> that Kathy loved Jesus.	apparent
8.	argument	I could not present a valid <u>argument</u> to uphold my view.	argument
9.	athlete	Edward's daily training made him a competitive <u>athlete</u>.	athlete
10.	believe	Thomas would not <u>believe</u> Christ had risen until he saw Him in person.	believe
11.	benefited	The new translation <u>benefited</u> my understanding tremendously.	benefited
12.	business	The town's <u>business</u> district has experienced much growth.	business
13.	existence	The <u>existence</u> of sin must be realized for salvation.	existence
14.	familiar	Are you <u>familiar</u> with the book of Malachi?	familiar
15.	finally	After waiting months for the snow, I <u>finally</u> went skiing.	finally
16.	foreign	This year our <u>foreign</u> exchange student was from Sweden.	foreign
17.	fulfill	Russell did not <u>fulfill</u> the company's requirements.	fulfill
18.	government	Our country's president has advisors to help him with <u>government</u> policies.	government
19.	grammar	Mrs. Nelson made sure her English class used correct <u>grammar</u>.	grammar
20.	height	The redwood forest has trees reaching a <u>height</u> of 200 feet.	height
21.	independent	Although physically connected, the two businesses were <u>independent</u> of each other.	independent
22.	intelligence	During the first part of the year, we were given <u>intelligence</u> tests.	intelligence

LIFEPAC TEST cont...

23.	personally	Theresa became personally involved with her Bible class.	personally
24.	primitive	There are still primitive tribes in the world who do not know Jesus Christ.	primitive
25.	procedure	It was a simple procedure to follow.	procedure
26.	curiosity	Ruth's curiosity was satisfied when she met her new neighbors.	curiosity
27.	receive	During the summer, our lodge did not receive guests.	receive
28.	repetition	Mrs. Hahn used repetition as a learning device.	repetition
29.	restaurant	The deserted highway did not indicate a restaurant for miles.	restaurant
30.	proceed	When our guide told us to proceed, we were very happy.	proceed
31.	deceive	Judas tried to deceive Jesus but failed.	deceive
32.	definite	The apostles were very definite in teaching Jesus' word.	definite
33.	desperate	We made one last desperate attempt to cross the river.	desperate
34.	dinosaurs	There were many replicas of this country's dinosaurs in the museum.	dinosaurs
35.	discipline	It was difficult to discipline the class after the party.	discipline
36.	dissatisfied	The Bible teaches us to live our lives for Jesus and not be dissatisfied.	dissatisfied
37.	doesn't	Nancy doesn't attend our church since she moved.	doesn't
38.	embarrass	It is unkind to intentionally embarrass someone.	embarrass
39.	environment	The world's environment has changed drastically since the time of Christ.	environment
40.	exaggerate	When Gene drew a caricature, he would exaggerate the features.	exaggerate
41.	grammatical	My book review came back with no grammatical errors.	grammatical
42.	misspelled	How often have you misspelled a word answer?	misspelled
43.	necessary	I find it necessary to do warm-up exercises before jogging.	necessary
44.	niece	My small niece loves to visit the zoo.	niece
45.	ninth	Carmel's name was ninth on the list.	ninth

ALTERNATE LIFEPAC TEST

1. nowadays   Nowadays television is an important communication medium.   nowadays
2. occasionally   Occasionally I like to have my friend over for dinner.   occasionally
3. occurrence   The river flooding is a natural occurrence in our part of the country.   occurrence
4. omission   Leaving out the most important point was a serious omission.   omission
5. optimistic   We were very optimistic about the upcoming project.   optimistic
6. parallel   Fifth Avenue runs parallel to Main Street.   parallel
7. perceive   I perceive that something has upset you.   perceive
8. sophomore   Henry was excited at the thought of becoming a sophomore.   sophomore
9. strength   Do you have enough strength to lift 150 pounds?   strength
10. tendency   I have the tendency to oversleep in the morning.   tendency
11. twelfth   My father was only the twelfth man in the nation to receive that degree.   twelfth
12. unnecessary   It is unnecessary to repeat your address on the form.   unnecessary
13. usually   I usually get up every day at six o'clock.   usually
14. vacuum   Saturday morning I have to vacuum the carpet.   vacuum
15. hymn   Everyone chose their favorite hymn for church Sunday.   hymn
16. climb   My friends and I have our favorite places to hike and climb.   climb
17. aisle   The bride walked nervously down the aisle.   aisle
18. calm   Bob remains calm in almost any situation.   calm
19. answer   Pat did not reach the phone in time to answer the call.   answer
20. condemn   The jury was ready to condemn him without hearing all the facts.   condemn
21. courtesy   Out of courtesy Tom held the door open for his mother.   courtesy
22. debt   In old England you could go to jail if you did not pay a debt.   debt
23. doubt   Why did Thomas the Apostle doubt the resurrection of Jesus?   doubt

ALTERNATE LIFEPAC TEST cont…

24.	ghost	In Dickens' "Christmas Carol," the ghost of Jacob Marley changed Scrooge's life.	ghost
25.	guess	Can you guess where we're going on vacation?	guess
26.	handsome	The handsome tennis player won all of his matches.	handsome
27.	island	The island of Maui is part of the beautiful state of Hawaii.	island
28.	knife	I keep my meat carving knife very sharp.	knife
29.	knight	Sir Lancelot was a knight in King Arthur's court.	knight
30.	knot	In macramé, each knot you tie is part of the design.	knot
31.	lamb	At the zoo, we saw a small lamb being fed from a bottle.	lamb
32.	listen	The apostles were graced by being able to listen to Jesus speak.	listen
33.	mortgage	Theresa's parents were happy to learn their mortgage was completely paid.	mortgage
34.	muscle	Your heart is a muscle that needs exercise to keep it healthy.	muscle
35.	palm	Hearts of palm is a delicious salad food.	palm
36.	pneumonia	Severe colds can often lead to pneumonia.	pneumonia
37.	scene	The ocean scene on the coast of California was breathtaking.	scene
38.	sign	The cross is used as symbol or sign of a Christian.	sign
39.	solemn	The inauguration of our president is a solemn occasion.	solemn
40.	subtle	There was a subtle change in my friend's face.	subtle
41.	thumb	Our thumb is crucial to our physical dexterity.	thumb
42.	Wednesday	Wednesday is usually considered the middle of the week.	Wednesday
43.	yacht	Someday I'd like to sail the seas on a fine yacht.	yacht
44.	familiar	Are you familiar with the Book of First Samuel?	familiar
45.	procedure	The assembly procedure was announced yesterday.	procedure

LIFEPAC TEST

1.	believe	Matthew 9:28 says, "Believe ye that I am able to do this?"	believe
2.	conscience	My conscience will not allow me to do that.	conscience
3.	counterfeit	The counterfeit painting was discovered by the museum.	counterfeit
4.	experience	The experience I gained as a camp counselor was invaluable.	experience
5.	height	The temperatures at the height of the summer average 112°.	height
6.	heirloom	This chest is a family heirloom that was made by my great-grandfather.	heirloom
7.	lei	Our greeters presented us each with an orchid lei.	lei
8.	mischievous	The mischievous boy was apprehended by the storekeeper.	mischievous
9.	perceive	The deer was able to perceive our presence.	perceive
10.	resilient	A sponge cloth is a very resilient piece of material.	resilient
11.	siege	The army laid siege to the city.	siege
12.	sovereignty	The king's sovereignty was not questioned.	sovereignty
13.	surveillance	The FBI had the suspect under surveillance.	surveillance
14.	affect	The radiation poisoning will affect several people.	affect
15.	already	The ship has already departed from the harbor.	already
16.	ascent	The jet developed engine trouble on its ascent.	ascent
17.	complement	The ship's entire complement came to attention.	complement
18.	counsel	The counsel I received from my pastor helped me through a difficult time in my life.	counsel
19.	holy	God told Moses to remove his shoes for he was on holy ground.	holy
20	niece	My niece will be attending Southwestern in the fall.	niece
21.	principal	The inquiry was made by the principal of the school.	principal
22.	raze	A tornado will raze a building within minutes.	raze
23.	scent	The skunk's scent permeated the air.	scent
24.	weather	The weather on Catalina Island was gorgeous.	weather

LIFEPAC TEST cont...

25.	wholly	Accept Christ <u>wholly</u> in your life.	wholly
26.	annihilate	Conservationists make sure we do not <u>annihilate</u> plant and animal life.	annihilate
27.	calendar	Our <u>calendar</u> is based upon the Roman calendar.	calendar
28.	Christianity	<u>Christianity</u> is the belief and worship of Christ based on the Scriptures.	Christianity
29.	conference	The Sunday school <u>conference</u> was sponsored by our church.	conference
30.	guarantee	The warranty will <u>guarantee</u> all phases of repair.	guarantee
31.	interrupt	Excuse me, I did not mean to <u>interrupt</u>.	interrupt
32.	deceit	Satan is the author of <u>deceit</u>.	deceit
33.	laboratory	Madam Curie's <u>laboratory</u> was a dilapidated shed.	laboratory
34.	opportunity	John was grateful for the <u>opportunity</u> to serve Christ.	opportunity
35.	prerogative	It is the judges <u>prerogative</u> to grant leniency.	prerogative
36.	recurring	Richard was plagued by a <u>recurring</u> pain in his arm.	recurring
37.	reference	Compile a list of all the books and articles you use as a <u>reference</u>.	reference
38.	restaurant	The new Italian <u>restaurant</u> is opening soon.	restaurant
39.	separate	John and Tim are on <u>separate</u> teams.	separate
40.	thoroughly	Larry's portrayal of Caesar was <u>thoroughly</u> convincing.	thoroughly
41.	accessible	The road is <u>accessible</u> from the north rim.	accessible
42.	confident	Our pastor was <u>confident</u> that our prayers would be answered.	confident
43.	desirable	A <u>desirable</u> vacation consists of a fishing rod, a cool mountain stream, and trout.	desirable
44.	elegant	The garden wedding was <u>elegant</u>.	elegant
45.	extravagant	The <u>extravagant</u> floral display greatly enhanced the chapel.	extravagant
46.	infallible	We realized that the computer was not <u>infallible</u>.	infallible
47.	irrelevant	The witness's testimony was <u>irrelevant</u>.	irrelevant
48.	lieutenant	The young <u>lieutenant</u> was commended for his heroism.	lieutenant
49.	permissible	Riding motorcycles in the reserve is not <u>permissible</u>.	permissible

LIFEPAC TEST cont...

50.	pre-existent	A butterfly in its pre-existent state is a caterpillar.	pre-existent
51.	significant	There has been a significant rise in gasoline prices.	significant
52.	supplement	Patti takes vitamins to supplement her diet.	supplement
53.	unstable	The bridge was unstable after the floods.	unstable
54.	arctic	The arctic weather was very unusual for our state.	arctic
55.	arrangement	The arrangement was written by our minister of music.	arrangement
56.	eighth	Our seats for the concert are in the eighth row.	eighth
57.	guarantee	In order to guarantee the accommodations, a deposit is required.	guarantee
58.	inhibition	Frank's inhibition about his height was totally unfounded.	inhibition
59.	isthmus	The isthmus was blackened by the oil spill.	isthmus
60.	maligned	Sherry asked for forgiveness because she maligned Alice.	maligned
61.	mortgage	The mortgage rate for the house is nine per cent.	mortgage
62.	pneumonia	After the operation the doctors watched for pneumonia.	pneumonia
63.	poignant	The reporter asked the candidate very poignant questions.	poignant
64.	rhyme	Free verse poetry does not necessarily rhyme.	rhyme
65.	solemn	The solemn look on his face made us realize something was amiss.	solemn
66.	whether	We do not know whether he went back to the ranch or to the store.	whether
67.	abbreviation	The abbreviation for attorney is "Atty."	abbreviation
68.	apostrophe	The apostrophe follows the "s" in the plural form.	apostrophe
69.	auxiliary	The auxiliary generator will provide lighting if the main one goes out.	auxiliary
70.	capitalization	Capitalization must be used when writing the name of a town.	capitalization
71.	communication	The communication center at the rangers station is very important.	communication
72.	contraction	The contraction can't is formed from the words can and not.	contraction

LIFEPAC TEST cont...

73.	diction	The British have wonderful diction.	diction
74.	gesture	It was a nice gesture of Susan's to help.	gesture
75.	hyphen	A hyphen is required in the phrase "self-addressed envelope."	hyphen
76.	library	The church library now has an extensive tape listing.	library
77.	narrative	The narrative gave an exciting account of the rescue.	narrative
78.	possessive	Write the possessive form of the word they.	possessive
79.	quotation marks	The title is usually in all caps and in quotation marks.	quotation marks
80.	syllable	The accent is on the first syllable.	syllable

ALTERNATE LIFEPAC TEST

1.	alien	The man must register because he is an alien.	alien
2.	ceiling	The ceiling in the old barn collapsed during the storm.	ceiling
3.	controversies	The controversies surrounding congressional expenditures led to an investigation.	controversies
4.	convenience	Living so close to school is a great convenience.	convenience
5.	forfeit	Due to a lack of sufficient players, the team had to forfeit.	forfeit
6.	freight	The fruit was shipped in the freight car.	freight
7.	heinous	Who would believe such a heinous crime could occur in these times!	heinous
8.	kaleidoscope	The forest was a kaleidoscope of colors.	kaleidoscope
9.	medieval	The medieval sword was originally owned by King Arthur.	medieval
10.	mischievous	The mischievous boy was apprehended by the storekeeper.	mischievous
11.	receipt	In receipt for the cake, I gave John a brownie.	receipt
12.	seize	The pickpocket tried to seize the woman's purse.	seize
13.	sovereignty	The king's sovereignty was not questioned.	sovereignty
14.	surveillance	The FBI had the suspect under surveillance.	surveillance
15.	aisle	The grocery aisle was jammed with people.	aisle
16.	altogether	That is an altogether different subject, Senator!	altogether
17.	chord	The chord was very dissonant.	chord
18.	colonel	The court martial of the colonel proved him guilty.	colonel
19.	corps	Our town's drum and bugle corps won first place in competition.	corps
20.	except	Everyone is ready for the trip except Jennifer.	except
21.	isle	We were shipwrecked on a deserted isle.	isle
22.	neigh	The boy made a sound like the neigh of a horse.	neigh
23.	personnel	The personnel director at summer camp is our pastor's wife.	personnel
24.	principal	The inquiry was made by the principal of the school.	principal

ALTERNATE LIFEPAC TEST cont...

25. racquet — My new racquet cracked when I ran into the wall. — racquet

26. reign — During the reign of George the III, America gained its independence. — reign

27. sleigh — On Christmas Day we always go for a sleigh ride. — sleigh

28. whether — We must leave at ten whether he has arrived or not. — whether

29. acknowledge — In order to be saved, you must first acknowledge your sins. — acknowledge

30. burglary — A burglary occurred yesterday but the thieves were apprehended. — burglary

31. Christianity — Christianity is the belief and worship of Christ based on the Scriptures. — Christianity

32. deceit — Satan is the author of deceit. — deceit

33. imperative — It is imperative that you reach Mr. Cunningham. — imperative

34. involuntary — Blinking is an involuntary action. — involuntary

35. kidnapped — The kidnapped heiress was ransomed and released. — kidnapped

36. omitting — Omitting his name was an error on my part. — omitting

37. picnicker — The picnicker was bothered by a swarm of bees. — picnicker

38. recurring — Richard was plagued by a recurring pain in his arm. — recurring

39. restaurant — The new Italian restaurant is opening soon. — restaurant

40. tentative — The tentative schedule is posted. — tentative

41. Wednesday — The social is planned for Wednesday afternoon. — Wednesday

42. amiable — I met the most amiable chap while strolling along the wharf. — amiable

43. covenant — Genesis 6:18 says "But with thee will I establish my covenant...." — covenant

44. efficient — Consumers today are purchasing fuel-efficient cars. — efficient

45. excusable — Impassable roads is an excusable absence from class. — excusable

46. hesitant — Patti was hesitant to walk in the ocean because of the jellyfish. — hesitant

47. irrelevant — The witness's testimony was irrelevant. — irrelevant

ALTERNATE LIFEPAC TEST cont...

48. obedient — Young people should be <u>obedient</u> to their parents. — obedient

49. pertinent — The officer's testimony was very <u>pertinent</u> to the case. — pertinent

50. responsible — The counselors are <u>responsible</u> for the meeting. — responsible

51. somnolent — Our pastor never gives a <u>somnolent</u> sermon! — somnolent

52. unpleasant — Cleaning up the barn is sometimes an <u>unpleasant</u> task. — unpleasant

53. vigilant — Mary kept a <u>vigilant</u> watch over Suzie when she was ill. — vigilant

54. acquire — The team was happy to <u>acquire</u> the new player. — acquire

55. arrangement — The <u>arrangement</u> was written by our minister of music. — arrangement

56. disguise — Aunt Jenny tried to <u>disguise</u> her voice on the phone. — disguise

57. exhausted — Jim was <u>exhausted</u> after softball practice and three games of racquetball. — exhausted

58. government — The <u>government</u>-controlled experiment was successful. — government

59. inhibition — Frank's <u>inhibition</u> about his height was successful. — inhibition

60. lightning — Is it possible for a man to be struck by <u>lightning</u> and still survive? — lightning

61. mathematician — Plato was a renowned <u>mathematician</u>. — mathematician

62. pneumonia — After the operation the doctors watched for <u>pneumonia</u>. — pneumonia

63. psychology — The <u>psychology</u> class will meet in the west wing. — psychology

64. scissors — The <u>scissors</u> are in my desk. — scissors

65. undoubtedly — The tornado is <u>undoubtedly</u> heading this way. — undoubtedly

66. writhe — Jennifer began to <u>writhe</u> in her chair in discomfort. — writhe

67. antonym — Write the <u>antonym</u> in the space provided. — antonym

68. asterisk — Additional information is available by the <u>asterisk.</u> — asterisk

69. capitalization — <u>Capitalization</u> must be used when writing the name of a town. — capitalization

ALTERNATE LIFEPAC TEST cont...

70.	communication	The communication center at the rangers station is very important.	communication
71.	determiners	The men and women of the jury are the determiners of innocence or guilt.	determiners
72.	formal	The formal congressional hearing will be held in May.	formal
73.	homonym	A word that sounds like another but is spelled differently is called a homonym.	homonym
74.	italics	The name of the pastor is printed in italics on the bulletin.	italics
75.	modifier	What is the modifier in the sentence?	modifier
76.	parenthesis	The typist left off one parenthesis.	parenthesis
77.	prefix	The prefix re- in the word *reappear* indicates *to appear again*.	prefix
78.	suffix	What is the suffix in the word extensively?	suffix
79.	syllable	The accent is on the first syllable.	syllable
80.	indebtedness	Gerald's indebtedness to Shawna was apparent.	indebtedness

T E S T S

Reproducible Tests
for use with the Language Arts
800 Teacher's Guide

Name _____

Answer *true* or *false* (each answer, 1 point).
1. _____ Communication is the first function of language.
2. _____ Prefixes cannot have semantic meaning.
3. _____ The spelling of a prefix is sometimes changed so that it fits more easily with the root.
4. _____ Analogies can be formed by using synonyms.
5. _____ The ending 's is an inflection.

Complete the analogies. Write the *letter* for the answer on each line (each answer, 2 points).
6. *Egg* is to *omelet* as _____ is to *butter*.
   a. bread   c. knife
   b. milk   d. sandwich
7. *Head* is to *hat* as _____ is to *glove*.
   a. finger   c. hand
   b. foot   d. elbow
8. *Cold* is to *hot* as _____ is to *summer*.
   a. snow   c. winter
   b. rain   d. ice
9. *Pencil* is to *paper* as _____ is to *meat*.
   a. beef   c. animal
   b. skin   d. knife

Match these items (each answer, 2 points).
10. _____ affix
11. _____ *-ness*
12. _____ categorizing
13. _____ *pre-*
14. _____ silent *e*
15. _____ facial expression

a. critical thinking
b. prefix
c. nonverbal message
d. prefix or suffix
e. movements
f. hope
g. suffix

Write the letter for the correct answer on each line (each answer, 2 points).

16.   The smallest meaningful unit of language structure is called a _____.
    a. suffix   c. prefix
    b. affix   d. morpheme

17.   An affix is a_____.
    a. root   c. prefix or suffix
    b. prefix   d. suffix

18.   Common relationships can be discovered by _____.
    a. definitions   c. analogies
    b. sentences   d. synonyms

19.   The most important listening courtesy is _____.
    a. taking notes   c. memorization
    b. attentiveness   d. following directions

20.   Sequence means _____.
    a. order   c. direction
    b. listing   d. advance

21.   Nonverbal communication is often used because it is _____.
    a. interesting   c. appreciated
    b. easy   d. necessary

Answer these questions (each answer, 5 points).

22.   How is nonverbal communication used for the deaf? _____

23.   What is an interjection? _____

24.   What are root words? _____

Complete these lists (each answer, 3 points).

25.   List three emotions that the face can express.

a.   _____

b.   _____

c.   _____

26.   List three groups of people that use hand signals.

a.   _____

b.   _____

c.   _____

Complete this activity (this answer, 5 points).

27.   Explain the way to give directions orally.

_____

_____

_____

60
/75

Date _____

Score _____

Name _____

Match these items (each answer, 2 points).

1. _____ adverb
2. _____ communication
3. _____ Indo-European
4. _____ Hellenic
5. _____ reflexive pronoun
6. _____ analytical
7. _____ dialect
8. _____ verb
9. _____ noun
10. _____ Aramaic
11. _____ philologist
12. _____ dominion

a. refers to subject
b. scientist who studies languages
c. logical
d. person, place, or thing
e. language spoken by mountaineers
f. Sanskrit
g. the language Jesus spoke
h. supreme authority
i. expresses state of being
j. modifies adverbs, verbs, adjectives
k. predecessor of Greek
l. European parent languages
m. exchange of ideas

Complete this statement (this item, 3 points).

13. Aramaic, the language Jesus spoke, belongs to the _____ family.

List two vivid adjectives for each of the following nouns (each answer, 3 points).

14. mountain   a. _____   b. _____
15. party   a. _____   b. _____
16. child   a. _____   b. _____
17. park   a. _____   b. _____
18. program   a. _____   b. _____

Write the part of speech of each italicized word on the line (each answer, 3 points).

19. The laundry was soaked by the *rainstorm*. _____

20. We waited for *him* at the corner. _____

21. He will attend a *small* college. _____

22. He walked very *slowly*. _____

23. He had trouble crossing the *busy* road. _____

24. The congregational *sang* a rousing anthem. _____

25. The branches *swayed* in the breeze. _____

26. They had to *cancel* the service because of snow. _____

27. Our *organist* is a very talented musician. _____

28. The boy looked *sadly* at his broken wagon. _____

Answer these questions (each answer, 5 points).

29. What is language? _____

_____

_____

30. Why is language so important to man? _____

_____

_____

31. How do dialects develop? _____

_____

_____

32. What is the difference between High German and Low German?

_____

_____

_____

86 / 107

Date _____

Score _____

Name _____

Punctuate these sentences where necessary and tell why punctuation is needed (each answer, 3 points).

1. Have you ever read *Moby Dick* a book about a white whale?

   _____

   _____

2. I climbed seven flights of stairs in ten minutes Mother took the elevator and had to wait for me at the top.

   _____

   _____

3. I would like to go to the park with you but my bicycle is broken.

   _____

   _____

4. The ants flies and the light rain everything seemed to go wrong on our camping trip last week.

   _____

   _____

5. Waiting for the girl to take his order Jimmy hungrily studied the menu.

   _____

   _____

6. The room what a mess had been searched by the intruder.

   _____

   _____

7. Although he had only been there five minutes Dave left their house.

   _____

   _____

8. Mr. Brown offered a reward to the boy or girl bringing in the most aluminum cans therefore Frank and I have been picking up cans in the park all morning.

   _____

   _____

9. A good pizza should contain the following ingredients cheese, tomato sauce, Italian sausage, olives, and spices.

    _____

    _____

10. Walter Jamison an outstanding businessman and a devout Christian has been elected president of the local businessmen's club.

    _____

    _____

Complete these statements (each answer, 3 points).

11. A period is generally used to end a. _____ and b. _____ sentences.

12. A question mark is used to end a (n) _____ sentence.

13. A dash is used to show _____ .

14. A colon generally appears _____ .

15. A word ending in *-d*, *-t*, *-ed*, *-en*, or *-ing* is a _____

    _____ .

Match these items (each answer, 2 points).

16. _____ genre

17. _____ expository

18. _____ theses

19. _____ formal essay

20. _____ informal essay

a. descriptive
b. having a light, humorous style
c. explanatory
d. a type or form
e. serious in nature
f. states a theory, belief, or opinion about a topic

List these items (each answer, 3 points).

21. List four characteristics of a formal essay.

a. _____

b. _____

c. _____

d. _____

22. List four characteristics of an informal essay.

a. _____

b. _____

c. _____

d. _____

23. List three methods an author may use to develop his essay.

a. _____

b. _____

c. _____

Answer this question (this answer, 5 points).

24. Where is the purpose of an essay generally stated?

_____

_____

77 / 96

Date _____

Score _____

Name _____

Complete these statements (each answer, 3 points).

1. *Roget's International Thesaurus* contains many _____ .
2. A straight, horizontal line placed over a vowel to show its sound or pronunciation is called a _____ .
3. Words that are opposite in meanings are called _____ .
4. The words *silent* and *talkative* are _____ .
5. *Admire* is a synonym for _____ .
6. English that is spoken or written by mature people is called

    _____ .

Answer *true* or *false* (each answer, 1 point).

7. _____ A shortened form for a word, such as *couldn't* for *could not*, is a contraction.
8. _____ An accent mark shows the part of the word that receives special emphasis or force when we pronounce it.
9. _____ The diacritical mark called a breve is used to show that a vowel has a long sound.
10. _____ Standard English never changes.
11. _____ The expression *had ought to* is never acceptable.

Match these items (each answer, 2 points).

12. _____ contraction
13. _____ slang
14. _____ commentator
15. _____ night/knight
16. _____ thesaurus
17. _____ macron

a. homonyms
b. indicates long vowel sound
c. shortened form of a word
d. book of synonyms
e. news reporter
f. unacceptable vocabulary
g. antonyms

Complete these statements with the correct words (each answer, 2 points).

18. If he needs money he (had ought to, should) _____ work for it.
19. The (affect, effect) _____ of the earthquake was felt several hundred miles away.

20. She did not come to the party because her friends forgot to send her an (invite, invitation) _____ .

21. Please (sit, set) _____ down and rest for a few minutes.

22. My brother (taught, learned) _____ me how to do algebra.

Rewrite these sentences substituting for the italicized words the indicated type of word (each answer, 3 points).

23. He finished his geography *coarse* in one semester. (homonym)

_____

_____

24. Lynn *dislikes* asparagus in salads. (antonym)

_____

_____

25. Jerry will be *there* in an hour. (antonym)

_____

_____

26. We had a *nice* time at the fair. (synonym)

_____

_____

Answer *true* or *false* (each answer, 1 point).

27. _____ If the dictionary marks *gnarly* (när' le), it should rhyme with Charlie.

28. _____ *Lichenous* (li' ku nus) should sound like a phrase describing the way someone feels about us.

29. _____ *Esophageal* (e' su faj' e ul) should sound like a phrase describing someone surfing on an eel.

Complete this activity (this answer, 5 points).

30. Give five suggestions for following written directions.

_____

_____

_____

_____

_____

_____

_____

_____

| 52 / 65 |

Date _____

Score _____

Name _____

Complete these activities (each answer, 3 points).

1. Write a synonym for each word.

   a. mistake   _____

   b. ask   _____

   c. hole   _____

2. Write an antonym for each word.

   a. descend   _____

   b. healthy   _____

   c. tasteless   _____

3. Write a homonym for each word.

   a. their   _____

   b. hare   _____

   c. main   _____

Complete these statements (each answer, 3 points).

4. Three things the Bible says about our speech include a. _____ ,
   b. _____ , and c._____ .

5. Three of the qualities a good speaker should have include
   a. _____ , b. _____ , and
   c._____ .

6. The apostrophe is used to a. _____ and to
   b._____ .

7. The words *concave* and *convex* are _____ .

8. A speech about your own life is considered _____ .

9. Underlining should be used wherever _____ are used in
   print.

Answer *true* or *false* (each answer, 1 point).

10. _____ Numbers over 100 are usually spelled out.
11. _____ Dates are not usually spelled out.
12. _____ Numbers should be spelled out for mathematics.
13. _____ The names of short poems should be italicized.
14. _____ The word *pronounciation* is spelled correctly.
15. _____ The word *humerous* is misspelled.
16. _____ To avoid errors when dividing a word at the end of a line, consult a dictionary.

Complete these activities (each answer, 3 points).

17. Abbreviate these words.
   a. avenue _____
   b. medical doctor _____
   c. reverend _____
18. Place capital letters correctly in the sentence.
   a. lisa lang became homecoming queen.

   _____

   b. the bible says god created heaven and earth.

   _____

19. Hyphenate these words.
   a. crisscrossed _____
   b. sixty three hundred _____
   c. two thirds _____
20. Write the singular possessive.
   a. son-in-law _____
   b. Tim and Ed _____
21. Write the plural possessive
   a. father-in-law _____
   b. hero _____
22. Place parentheses in the proper places.
   a. Jimmy Carter is 1. President, 2. a husband, and 3. a father.
   b. In 1941 I was only two years old Pearl Harbor was bombed.
23. Write contractions for the following words.
   a. she is _____
   b. we are _____
   c. were not _____
   d. is not _____

Circle the correct word (each answer, 2 points).

24.   Will you accept/except the telephone call?

25.   The affects/effects of that disease can be serious.

26.   She appreciated the complement/compliment.

102 / 127

Date _____
Score _____

Name _____

Match these items (each answer, 2 points).

1. _____ Beowulf
2. _____ Chaucer
3. _____ Alfred
4. _____ Byrd
5. _____ Stuart
6. _____ the "Hump"
7. _____ Grendel
8. _____ gnomes
9. _____ Danelaw
10. _____ Sutton Hoo

a. an Anglo-Saxon king
b. wise sayings
c. little elves in an epic poem
d. a man-eating monster
e. the hero of an epic
f. the site of a ship burial
g. a twentieth-century explorer
h. an area of England given to the Danes
i. a country school teacher
j. a fourteenth-century writer
k. a dangerous area near the South Pole

Write the letter for the correct answer on each line (each answer, 2 points).

11. The year 1066 is important because it marks the date of the_____.
   a. Norman Conquest
   b. end of Roman occupation
   c. birth of Chaucer
   d. death of Alfred

12. Before the year AD 55 Britain had been occupied by the_____.
   a. Romans
   b. Celts
   c. Anglo-Saxons
   d. Normans

13. The earliest epic in Old English is _____.
   a. the *Canterbury Tales*
   b. the "Ruin"
   c. Sutton Hoo
   d. *Beowulf*

14. The Old English word modor means _____.
   a. modern
   b. odor
   c. mother
   d. murder

15. During the seventh and eighth centuries, monasteries were _____.
   a. educational and cultural centers
   b. important political establishments
   c. military centers for the Normans
   d. unimportant

16. Lines of verse having words beginning with the same initial sounds are considered _____.
   a. alliterative
   b. inflected
   c. dialectic
   d. precipitous

17. A major rule in using coordination is that a writer must coordinate sentence elements of _____.
   a. similar or equal usage
   b. lesser importance
   c. different types
   d. conditional relationships

18. An adjective clause is usually introduced by a _____.
    a. coordinating conjunction   c. conjunctive adverb
    b. relative pronoun   d. reflexive pronoun
19. The flight to the South Pole began on _____.
    a. the Fourth of July   c. Christmas Eve
    b. Thanksgiving Day   d. Memorial Day
20. The title, "The Thread That Runs So True," came from _____.
    a. an old saying by the author's uncle
    b. a quilting pattern
    c. a Bible verse
    d. a game played by the hill children

Complete these statements (each answer, 3 points).
21. A clause that is necessary for identification of a word is called
    _____.
22. A clause that is less important than the main clause is _____.
23. The words *either...or* are _____.
24. A long narrative poem about the deeds of a hero is _____.
25. Anglo-Saxon (Old English) was a(n) _____ language; that
    is, it depended on a change of form in words to indicate grammatical
    relationships.
26. Time relationship, cause or reason relationship, purpose or result
    relationship, or condition relationship is shown by a(n) _____.
27. The words *whenever*, *whereas*, and *although* are _____.
28. The words *nevertheless*, *likewise*, and *consequently* are _____.
29. Another word for the story or account of someone or something is
    _____.
30. A story a person writes about his own life is a(n) _____.
31. The main idea of the author is generally called the _____ of
    the story.

Complete this activity (each answer, 3 points).
32. List three of the five elements of the autobiography.
    a. _____
    b. _____
    c. _____

66	
	82

Date _____
Score _____

Name _____

Match these items (each answer, 2 points).

1. _____ connotation
2. _____ symbol
3. _____ directive language
4. _____ denotation
5. _____ inference
6. _____ a word's context
7. _____ appeal to mass emotion
8. _____ oversimplification
9. _____ dishonest propaganda
10. _____ name calling

a. Mercedes equals wealth
b. car—a vehicle used for transportation
c. "What a feast!" (looking at the soggy meat loaf)
d. pumpkin—an affectionate term for someone
e. "He that believeth in me shall never die."
f. My daughter does care how our laundry smells!
g. but my opponent, J.J. Jones, allowed crime to rise 50 per cent last year
h. happiness comes to all people who give total allegiance to the State
i. all the deaths occurred near his neighborhood
j. "Just spray and wipe and your work is done!"
k. transition

Complete these statements (each answer, 3 points).

11. A good paragraph must be a. _____ and b. _____.
12 The sentence that summarizes the topic sentence in the long paragraph is called the _____.
13. A narrative paragraph uses dialogue to _____.
14. Descriptive writing appeals to the _____.
15. Most of the reading and writing you will do is _____.

Answer *true* or *false* (each answer, 1 point).

16. _____ The deductive method of reasoning is particular to general.
17. _____ Reasoning from particular to general is called inductive reasoning.
18. _____ A chronological paragraph would be best for a paper on acupuncture and surgery as healing methods.
19. _____ The best method in a contrast of two things would be a point-by-point discussion of differences.
20. _____ Spatial order is most effective when one is describing what he sees.

21. _____ Paragraph continuity of thought is one of the methods of unity.

22. _____ Pronouns are effective transitions because they have antecedents within the paragraph.

23. _____ Any transitional word seems to fit in at the beginning of a new paragraph.

24. _____ The difference between unity and coherence is that coherence is actually a part of unity.

25. _____ The word *coherence* means *to stick together*.

Write the letter of the correct answer on the line (each answer, 2 points).

26. The most important section of the paper is the _____.
    a. thesis   c. conclusion
    b. introduction   d. body

27. The thesis is _____.
    a. what you're proving   c. the transition
    b. the theme   d. both b and c

28. The best method for opening your composition is by _____.
    a. opening with particular (specific) statements to general ones
    b. stating your thesis first
    c. constructing it in triangular style
    d. opening with general to particular (specific)
    e. both a and b

29. The best way to organize a body of paragraphs on the Civil War would be with _____.
    a. reasons   c. incidents
    b. examples   d. all of these

30. The most effective way to organize your arguments is to _____.
    a. put the strongest first
    b. handle them all at once
    c. place the opposing arguments last
    d. place the strongest last

31. A transition word like *nevertheless* might be used to _____.
    a. illustrate   c. contrast
    b. add something   d. conclude

32. The purpose of transition words at the beginning of new paragraphs is to _____.
    a. tie the new one to the old
    b. maintain the reader's concentration
    c. maintain the unity of the new paragraph
    d. introduce a new subject

33. The length of the body of a composition _____.
     a. should be three to ten paragraphs
     b. depends on the conclusion
     c. is dependent upon the writer
     d. both b and c
34. The conclusion should _____.
     a. remain static
     b. be a separate, organized unit
     c. restate the thesis and body
     d. bridge the body to the introduction
35. To avoid a dull conclusion the writer should _____.
     a. give a good general statement for the reader to ponder at the end
     b. avoid just repeating the thesis word for word
     c. avoid just listing items from the body of the paper
     d. all of these

Write *RO* by each run-on sentence and *F* by each sentence fragment. Then rewrite each one as a complete sentence (each answer, 3 points).

36. Wherever his friends gather.   a. _____
     b. _____
37. Although I needed every eraser I could get.   a. _____
     b. _____
38. Waking up in the middle of the night and finding the lights out.
     a. _____
     b. _____
     _____
39. Knowledge of the Bible is essential for the Christian life, every
     Christian should read his daily.   a. _____
     b. _____
     _____
40. I really enjoyed the play after school today, I didn't even miss leaving at
     3:30.   a. _____
     b. _____
     _____
41. Aged and lonely after long years that she spent in the prison camp.
     a. _____
     b. _____
     _____

83 / 104

Date _____
Score _____

Name _____

Answer *true* or *false* (each answer, 1 point).
1. _____ Inferred meanings are exact.
2. _____ Exaggeration is a common figure of speech.
3. _____ Tone of voice and body actions are examples of literal meanings.
4. _____ To be a good listener it is not necessary to be able to give good advice.
5. _____ Everything you read in a magazine or newspaper is true.
6. _____ Slanted news tries to "sell" a viewpoint.
7. _____ You can tell if something is logical by the way it sounds.
8. _____ Makeup and size of the group are important when dealing with statistics.
9. _____ An atlas is a general source of information.
10. _____ A majority of Americans read a daily newspaper.

Match these items (each answer, 2 points).
11. _____ *Readers' Guide*
12. _____ gesture
13. _____ statistics
14. _____ figurative language
15. _____ nonfiction
16. _____ salutation
17. _____ literal meaning
18. _____ editorial
19. _____ propaganda
20. _____ heading

a. an article in a newspaper expressing opinion
b. conversation
c. attempts to inform, explain, define, analyze, interpret, or persuade
d. an index of magazine articles
e. the greeting following the inside address
f. factual numbers
g. implied meanings through the use of comparisons
h. exact words
i. techniques used to persuade the public
j. the writer's address and the date
k. meaningful body movements

Complete these statements (each answer, 3 points).

21.   Three kinds of personal letters include the a. _____,

     b. _____, and c. _____.

22.   Three types of business letters are the a. _____,

     b. _____, and c. _____.

23.   Eyewitness reports, diaries, letters, and interviews are examples of

     _____ sources.

24.   Four different figures of speech include a. _____,

     b. _____, c. _____, and d. _____.

25.   Reuters and AP are wire services that _____.

26.   The part of a business letter that is not a part of a personal letter is the

     _____.

Answer these questions (each answer, 5 points).

27.   How do newspapers and news magazines differ?

     _____

     _____

     _____

28.   What are the characteristics of a good listener?

     _____

     _____

     _____

63 / 79

Date _____

Score _____

Name _____

Match these items (each answer, 2 points).

1. _____ jargon
2. _____ double negative
3. _____ persuasion
4. _____ archaic
5. _____ antecedent
6. _____ dangling modifier
7. _____ assimilate
8. _____ inflect
9. _____ exposition
10. _____ elliptical

a. outdated
b. a clause having one or more words omitted
c. absorbed into
d. the social patterns characteristic of a certain people
e. specialized or technical language
f. to vary the pitch of the voice
g. states an opinion and the reasons supporting it, designed to convince
h. consists of two negative modifiers to the verb
i. a presentation of information
j. is usually attached to the wrong word or no word
k. must agree with the pronoun referring to it

Write *true* or *false* (each answer, 1 point).

11. _____ *Enunciation* refers to the uninflected spoken word.
12. _____ An important element of the pentad is the setting.
13. _____ Whenever a writer changes paragraphs he should shift from the first person to second.
14. _____ A prepositional phrase is a good example of an elliptical clause.
15. _____ Of these three words, *ammission*, *paralell*, and *exaggerate*, two are misspelled.
16. _____ The *mood* of a verb is the way an action or state of being is stated.
17. _____ The thesis introduces the purpose or direction of a report.
18. _____ A collective noun is always used with a singular verb.
19. _____ A good rule for using gestures is to be natural.
20. _____ Antecedents joined by *nor* or *or* must use a singular noun.

Complete these statements (each answer, 3 points).

21. A step-by-step examination of how something works is called

_____ .

22. To avoid confusion a modifier should be placed _____ .

23. One example of a dead language is _____.

24. Written English became respectable with the works of the great English poet _____.

25. In English the three moods of a verb are a. _____, b. _____, and c. _____.

26. A five point pattern for organizing a speech is called the _____.

27. The tracking of the history and development of a word from its earliest source is called _____.

28. Two ways words have come into English are a. _____ and b. _____.

29. Three necessary parts of a report are a. _____, b. _____, and c. _____.

Date _____

Score _____

Name _____

Match these items (each answer, 2 points).

1. _____ Indo-European
2. _____ dialect
3. _____ etymology
4. _____ documentation
5. _____ nonstandard
6. _____ acronym
7. _____ figures
8. _____ run-on
9. _____ comma-splice
10. _____ purchase request

a. proof of facts used in a theme
b. used for dates and addresses
c. a business letter
d. a personal letter
e. the parent language
f. two or more complete sentences joined by a comma
g. local characteristics of speech usually developed in an isolated geographic region
h. abbreviations used as words
i. the history of words
j. two or more sentences joined by excessive use of conjunctions
k. one of the two types of English

Complete these statements (each answer, 3 points).

11. The smallest meaningful unit of the English language is the _____.
12. A technique used for generating ideas to discuss or to write about is called _____.
13. The beginning sentence of a news article is called the _____.
14. Determining the meaning of an unfamiliar word by looking at the way the word is used in the sentence or paragraph is called using

    _____.
15. The type of noun used to name things you can see and touch is
    a. _____; the type of noun used to name qualities or ideas is b. _____.
16. Personal pronouns may be used as a. _____, b. _____, or c. _____.
17. Two types of personal compound pronouns are a. _____ and b. _____.
18. A dictionary should provide three types of information:
    a. _____, b. _____, and
    c. _____.
19. An essay should a. _____ or b. _____.
20. A news article should consist of _____.

Write *true* or *false* (each answer, 1 point).

21. _____ A colon often follows an independent clause that ends in a noun and signals that information is about to follow.

22. _____ Capitalize the first word in each sentence and all the words in the titles of books and songs.

23. _____ A thesaurus lists synonyms, antonyms, and homonyms for many different words.

24. _____ A good paragraph should contain many different ideas, so that the reader will be interested.

25. _____ A clincher statement can conclude a paragraph or provide a transition to the next paragraph.

26. _____ The word *counterfiet* is misspelled.

27. _____ The first dictionary ever published was written by Daniel Webster.

28. _____ Communication of ideas through pantomime depends upon posture, facial expressions, gestures, style of walking, clothing, and makeup.

29. _____ A thesis states the purpose or central idea of a theme or composition.

30. _____ Two types of essays are standard and nonstandard.

Answer these questions (each answer, 5 points).

31. What are the basic purposes of speeches? _____
_____
_____

32. What is sequence and what are the various types of sequence you have studied? _____
_____
_____
_____

33. What makes up the autobiography? _____
_____
_____

Date _____

Score _____

ANSWER KEYS

SECTION ONE

1.1   unlock meanings

1.2   root

1.3   a.   prefixes
       b.   suffixes

1.4   at the beginning of words

1.6   prefix

1.7   a.   un-
       b.   -ist
       c.   syn-
       d.   un-
       e.   mis-
       f.   -lish
       g.   re-, -tion
       h.   -less
       i.   -ward, -ness
       j.   ex-
       k.   in-, -ious
       l.   im-, -ant

1.8   a.   -es
       b.   noun
       c.   plural

1.9   a.   -ed
       b.   verb
       c.   past tense

1.10   a.   -ing
       b.   verb
       c.   participle

1.11   a.   -est
       b.   adjective
       c.   superlative

1.12   a.   -es
       b.   verb
       c.   present tense

1.13   a.   -'s
       b.   noun
       c.   possessive

1.14   a.   -t
       b.   verb
       c.   past tense

1.15   a.   -es
       b.   noun
       c.   plural

1.16   a.   -er
       b.   adjective
       c.   comparative

1.17   a.   beautiful
       b.   beauty

1.18   a.   holiness
       b.   holy

1.19   a.   unlocked
       b.   lock

1.20   a.   servant
       b.   serve

1.21   a.   reaction
       b.   act

1.22   a.   amazingly
       b.   amaze

1.23   a.   foresight
       b.   sight

1.24   a.   unreasonable
       b.   reason

1.25   a.   misinformation
       b.   inform

1.26   a.   auto
       b.   mobile

1.27   a.   tele
       b.   phone

1.28   a.   over
       b.   lap

1.29   a.   shell
       b.   fish

1.30   a.   camp
        b.   fire

1.31   a.   side
        b.   walk

1.32   hydro and phobia
1.33   speed and meter
1.34   weight
1.35   miracle
1.36   destroy
1.37   defense
1.38   vapor
1.39   grammar
1.40   fable
1.41   love
1.42   might
1.43   pepper and mint
1.44   penny
1.45   soft and speak
1.46   busy

1.47   a.   two
        b.   wheel

1.48   a.   within
        b.   wall

1.49   a.   distance
        b.   sight

1.50   a.   not
        b.   comfort

1.51   a.   across
        b.   carry
        c.   means of

1.52   every two weeks
1.53   between schools

1.54   to deprive of arms (weapons)
1.55   across the ocean
1.56   communicate over a distance
1.57   g, f, d, n
1.58   h, a
1.59   b, i, f
1.60   c, j, e
1.61   e, g, l, m
1.62   g, n, k
1.63   o, m, g

1.64 - 1.72   Answers may vary.
1.64   none
1.65   none
1.66   both
1.67   both
1.68   grammatical
1.69   none
1.70   semantic
1.71   none
1.72   semantic

1.73   Examples: Is it organic?
        Is it an animal?
        Does it have four legs?
1.74   Examples: flowers, flowering
        shrubs, shrubs, plants
1.75   Example: spices
1.76   Example: fabrics or materials
1.77   Examples: games or sports

1.78   Example: zoo animals

1.79   b. road
1.80   c. paper
1.81   d. migrate

1.82   c. shark
1.83   Examples:
   a. long, slender objects
   b. four-legged animals, mammals, domestic animals
   c. pans, kitchen utensils
   d. nouns
   e. dairy products
   f. things which can be sharpened
   g. female gender
1.84   Examples:

   a. nouns
   b. writing tools
   c. long slender objects
   d. pointed things
   e. things that erase
   f. wooden objects
   g. painted objects
1.85   brief - short, concise
   efficient
   field - a plot of land
   fiend
   fiery - containing or composed of fire
   freight
   friend - a person for whom one has regard or affection
   grief
   height - distance from base to top; stature
   heinous
   heirloom- anything that has been handed down through a family for generations
   kaleidoscope
   lei - a garland of flowers

leisure
medieval - belonging to, like, or characteristic of the Middle Ages
mischievous
neigh - the cry of a horse
neither
niece - the daughter of a brother, brother-in law, sister, or sister-in-law
perceive
pierce - to penetrate as with a pointed instrument
priest
reign - possession or exercise of royal power
seize
siege - act of surrounding a town with the intent of capturing it
sieve
sleigh - horse drawn vehicle with runners, for use on snow
surveillance
view - act of seeing, outlook
yield

1.86   b
1.87   a

1.88   a

1.89   c

1.90   b or d

1.91   d

1.92   b

1.93   d

1.94   d

SECTION TWO

2.1 teacher check. Example:

NAME

DATE

2.2 2
5
1
4
3

2.3 4
2
5
1
3

2.4 5
1
4
3
2

2.5 teacher check

2.6 Example: Tying shoes
a. Cross the laces.
b. Tuck one lace under the other.
c. Pull tight.
d. Make a loop in one lace.
e. Wrap the other lace around the base of the loop, keeping them separate with your fingers.
f. Make a second loop and bring it through the opening between the two laces.
g. Pull tight.

2.7 Hint: Answer should indicate that the desired result was not achieved.

2.8 attentiveness

2.9 sequence

2.10 repeat

2.11 a. Listen attentively.
b. Take notes.
c. Ask questions.

2.12 Example: To bake a cake, first assemble your ingredients. Preheat the oven to 350°. Grease and flour the pan. Mix the ingredients. Pour into pan. Bake for 35 minutes.

2.13 Example:
a. Assemble the ingredients.
b. Preheat the oven.
c. Grease and flour the pan.
d. Sift the dry ingredients, set aside.
e. Combine egg, milk, and sugar.
f. Add dry ingredients to egg mixture.
g. Bake.

2.14 Example: Directions for "Hangman" game. — Draw a figure seven. Make a set of steps coming down from the seven. Think of a word. Below the figure put as many blanks as the are letters in the word. Have me guess the letters in your word. For each letter I miss draw a body part (head, eye, arm, etc.). For each letter I guess correctly, fill in the blank in your word. Keep track of the letters I guess incorrectly. If I guess the word before I run out of letters or before you "hang" me, I'm the winner.

2.15 defamation

2.16 indelibly

2.17 babyish

2.18 tartness

2.19 picnicker
2.20 courageous

2.21 funniest
2.22 duly

2.23 ripping
2.24 bigger

2.25 a. admission
      b. admit
2.26 a. argument
      b. argue

2.27 a. Biblical
      b. Bible
2.28 a. Christianity
      b. Christ
2.29 a. courageous
      b. courage
2.30 a. deception
      b. deceive
2.31 a. defamation
      b. defame

2.32 a. duly
      b. due

2.33 a. expulsion
      b. expel

2.34 a. fabulous
      b. fable

2.35 a. government
      b. govern

2.36 a. grammatical
      b. grammar

2.37 a. happiness
      b. happy
2.38 a. heaviness
      b. heavy
2.39 a. honorable
      b. honor

2.40 a. inaccessible
      b. access

2.41 a. indelibly
      b. indelible

2.42 a. information
      b. inform

2.43 a. inspiration
      b. inspire
2.44 a. marriage
      b. marry
2.45 a. omitting
      b. omit
2.46 a. picnicker
      b. picnic
2.47 a. portable
      b. port
2.48 a. recurring
      b. occur
2.49 a. reference
      b. refer

2.50 a. referral
      b. refer

2.51 a. responsibility
      b. respond

2.52 a. scientifically
      b. science

2.53 a. spherical
      b. sphere

2.54 a. substitution
      b. substitute

2.55 1. portable
      2. expel
      3. information
      4. argument
      5. indelibly
      6. courageous
      7. sphere
      8. reference
      9. omitting
      10. ing
      11. referral
      12. marriage
      13. ment
      14. duly
      15. honor
      16. scientifically

SECTION THREE

(3.1 - 3.5): Examples

3.1 I don't care what anyone else wants. I'll please myself, no matter.

3.2 I'm too good to be with the group. I want to be set apart and respected.

3.3 I have no respect.

3.4 I want to make the best impression to get the job.

3.5 Who cares? I don't even like myself.

3.6 Any order:
   a. happiness
   b. sadness
   c. fear
   d. surprise
   e. anger
   f. curiosity
   g. disgust

3.7 Examples: emotions, embarrassment, happiness, sadness, fear, surprise, anger, curiosity, disgust

3.8 Examples:
   a. smiles - happiness
   b. frowns, grimaces - rejection
   c. sticking out tongue, rolling eyes - derogatory comments about something
   d. tightened lips, flexing jaw muscle - anger

3.9 a. no
   b. yes

3.10 teacher check

3.11 a. Example: Rather bent over, shoulders sagging, head down
   b. Example: Not interested in things around him; withdrawn; depressed
   c. Example: Slowly
   d. Answers will vary.

3.12 Examples; any order:
   a. shaking hands
   b. waving
   c. clapping
   d. praying

3.13 teacher check

3.14 teacher check

3.15 Examples; any order: sign language, sports signals, hand alphabet for deaf

3.16 Examples: distance communication where other methods won't work; Noisy areas

3.17 teacher check

3.18 teacher check

3.19 to say or do again and again; to repeat

3.20 distinguished; outstanding

3.21 to give an advance indication or suggestion of

3.22 results; consequences; especially unfavorable consequences

3.23 before the Flood

3.24 occurring every two years

3.25 occurring twice a year; half-yearly

3.26 a musical composition; an introductory performance or event

3.27 underground

3.28   aforementioned

aftermath

antediluvian

anti-intellectual

antislavery

antonym

biennial

departure

descend

foreshadow

inarticulate

inedible

interrupt

involuntary

non-English

nonmember

non nuclear

preeminent

prehistoric

prelude

pre-shrunk

reiterate

semiannual

subterranean

trans-Atlantic

transcontinental

transmission

unfriendly

SECTION ONE

1.1 Language separates man from the animals. It allows him to work with others by communicating even abstract ideas.

1.2

French	Spanish
a. la chaise	la silla
b. la lit	la cama
c. l'arbre	el arbol
d. la nourriture	la comida
e. la maitresse	el profesor
f. l' e'cole	la escuela
g. le livre	el libro
h. le pupitre	el escritorio

1.3 AF - Anglo-French
Dan. - Danish
Du. - Dutch
E - English
F, FR - French
G, Ger. - German
Gk. - Greek
Heb. - Hebrew
HG - High German
L, Lat - Latin
LG - Low German
MF - Middle French
OE - Old English
OF - Old French
OHG - Old High German
Sp - Spanish

1.4 Examples:
creek, crik, bayou, soda, pop, coke, y'all, yous guys

1.5 Example:
By studying the changes words in related languages such as English, Latin, and Greek have undergone, scientists can trace a word back to its original form.

1.6 Hint:
Trace from Indo-European to Proto-Germanic to West Germanic, Low German, Old English, and Middle English to Modern English.

1.7 a. Indo-European
b. Proto-Germanic
c. West Germanic
d. Low German
e. Old English
f. Middle English

1.8 th instead of t

1.9 Example:
Greek hepta is spelled with an h while the other forms for seven start with s. English uses th in mother (as does Celtic) while Greek, Latin, and Sanskrit use t. Only English has the gh combination (as in night).

1.10 West Germanic subdivided into Low German

1.11 stress

1.12 pitch

1.13 a. Latin
b. Celtic

1.14 a group of Indo -Europeans who settled in Greece
or the ancestors of the Greeks
(1.15 - 1.22) Examples:

1.15 Sherlock Holmes had an analytical mind.

1.16 There is a close correlation between climate and crops.

1.17 He knew many dialects.

1.18 The nearsighted spy could not distinguish his own coat from his enemy's.

1.19 The King had dominion over his subjects.

1.20 He was a linguist.

1.21 During the night a strange phenomenon occurred.

1.22 A philologist studies linguistics.

SECTION TWO

2.1   a. airplane
     b. dishwasher
     e. desk
     g. basket
     i. gentlemen
     k. gymnasium
     l. racquet
     m. mansion

2.2   A noun names a person, place, or thing.

2.3   Harold, songs

2.4   Patty, telephone

2.5   boys, tennis

2.6   girl, puddle

2.7   car, rain

2.8   students, school

2.9   his, She, them, She, she, they

2.10   Example:
One of the most beautiful stories in the Bible is that of Joseph. He was used by God to save his family from starvation. His brothers were insanely jealous of him. They sold him as a slave to travelers to Egypt. Arriving in Egypt, he worked as a servant for many years until Pharaoh summoned him to interpret a series of dreams. He rewarded Joseph by giving him a position managing the grain storage. In this position Joseph met his brothers when they came to buy grain. Joseph sent his brothers back for his father and the family was once more united.

2.11   whose   a. interrogative
       you   b. personal

2.12   those   demonstrative

2.13   it   a. personal
      itself   b. compound

2.14   that   a. relative
      you   b. personal

2.15   these   a. demonstrative
      theirs   b. possessive

2.16   which   a. interrogative
      yours   b. possessive

2.17   nobody   a. indefinite
      me   b. personal

2.18   I   a. personal
      you   b. personal

2.19   Hint: Check your paragraph for these things:
     a. used complete sentences
     b. used correct punctuation (capitalization and periods)
     c. each pronoun referred to a specific noun.

2.20   A pronoun replaces a noun.

2.21   buys, wants

2.22   will discuss

2.23   said, Let, be

2.24   said, Follow, will make

2.25   made

2.26-2.31 Examples:

2.26   threw

2.27   kicked

2.28   batted

2.29   saw

2.30   spotted

2.31   lost

2.32   Example:
The fifth grade cooperates best.

2.33 <u>Drifting</u> fog
  <u>narrow</u> <u>river</u> valleys
  <u>thick</u> forest
  <u>chill</u> mist
  <u>quiet</u> <u>little</u> farms
  <u>picturesque</u> countryside

2.34 Examples:
  a. well-dressed
  b. children's
  c. shaggy
  d. waiting
  e. slow
  f. ten
  g. expensive
  h. steep
  i. little
  j. huge
  k. meaty
  l. hungry

2.35 An adjective modifies a noun.

2.36 An adverb modifies a verb,
  adjective, or another adverb.

2.37 stealthily, eerily, nervously,
  fearfully, excitedly, sheepishly,
  immediately

Examples (2.38 - 2.47):

2.38 quickly
2.39 nervously
2.40 sneakily
2.41 boldly
2.42 noisily
2.43 straight
2.44 swiftly
2.45 politely
2.46 irritably
2.47 gleefully

(2.48 - 2.55) Examples
2.48 An auxiliary verb is a helping verb.

2.49 My coin collection is categorized by
  dates.

2.50 The United States is comprised of fifty
  states.

2.51 Buying a luxury car is extravagant.

2.52 Can you interpret this language?

2.53 The countryside was very picturesque.

2.54 Be specific in a business letter.

2.55 He worked steadily through the night.

2.56 extravagant

2.57 mansion

2.58 eliminate

2.59 gymnasium

2.60 noisily or heavily

2.61 microscope

2.62 racquet

2.63 starvation

2.64 sheepish

2.65 bicycle

2.66 tense

2.67 modifier

2.68 determiners

2.69 ACROSS

1. bicycle
7. stair
8. mice
9. retaliate
12. two
13. Noah
14. right
15. his
17. creative
18. him
19. steadily
21. them
22. grateful
24. gymnasium
27. noisily
28. padded
29. she
32. sheepish
35. letters
37. library
38. these
39. explain
42. pout
43. out
44. substitute
45. ether
46. he

DOWN

1. boast
2. curiously
3. communicate
4. excavate
5. slight
6. fast
10. extravagant
11. extremely
16. heavily
20. listless
23. hastily
25. up
26. mansion
30. he
31. whisper
32. scrape
33. excite
34. racquet
36. trees
40. ice
41. it
43. oh

SECTION THREE

3.1 Examples

a. gorgeous   e. fantastic
b. malevolent   f. rotted
c. shining   g. petite
d. gigantic   h. slight

3.2 Examples:
cozy, comfortable house
rainbow-like sunset
leafy, scarecrow tree
azure, brilliant sky
dark, gloomy forest
business-like man
beautiful, sleek cat
bulging, crowded bus

(3.3 - 3.5) Examples
3.3 all in white
3.4 paint peeling off

3.5 starched quite stiff
3.6 teacher check
Examples (3.7 - 3.11)
3.7 diligently
3.8 joyfully
3.9 swiftly

3.10 courageously

3.11 deftly

3.12 through the mud

3.13 with one finger
3.14 when it snows
3.15 to the lake
3.16 by following a recipe

3.17 - 3.21 Example: "You will make the team yet!" Mrs. Brown said encouragingly.

3.22 teacher check
Examples (3.23 - 3.52):

3.23 having a strong desire to achieve a particular goal

3.24 resentfully unable to forget pain

3.25 awkwardly

3.26 in a scornful manner

3.27 brilliant or splendid

3.28 without question

3.29 very sadly or drearily

3.30 terribly

3.31 irresistibly attractive

3.32 feeling that danger or evil is near

3.33 having done wrong

3.34 the condition of being well and not sick

3.35 showing anger at something unworthy or mean

3.36 hard to explain or understand

3.37 uneasily

3.38 having great value

3.39 thinking well of oneself

3.40 with haste

3.41 careless

3.42 trustworthy

3.43 uneasily

3.44 not smooth

3.45 quietly; without noise

3.46 scattered in drops or particles

3.47 happening or coming without notice; unexpectedly

3.48 having a dry feeling in the mouth caused by lack of water or liquids

3.49 shyly, rather fearfully

3.50 disagreeable; displeasing

3.51 rich

3.52 with wrath or great anger

3.53 teacher check

SECTION ONE

1.1 . . . book. It . . .
. . . Mississippi. The. . .
. . . adults. I . . .
. . . year. It . . .
. . . boring. Maybe. . .
. . . raft. You. . .
. . . Huck.

1.2 a. imperative
b. declarative

1.3 interrogative

1.4 strong, sudden feeling

1.5 . . . exercise. It . . .
. . . things. How. . .
. . . nature? You. . .
. . . day! Does. . .
. . . effort? Try. . .
. . . yourself. You'll. . .

1.6 within a sentence to connect independent clauses with another group of words

1.7 to tell the reader to pause, but not to stop

1.8 a. Use a comma before the conjunctions and, but, or, for, nor, so and yet.
b. Use a semicolon between the clauses without a conjunction.
c. Use a semicolon before a conjunctive adverb.

1.9 Examples:
a. Today is a beautiful day; the sun is shining.
b. We wanted to go hiking; however, it rained.
c. I like the Colorado Rockies, but I also like the Catskills.

1.10 . . . book, yet. . . .

1.11 . . . master; it. . . .

1.12 . . . postponed; therefore we. . .

1.13 . . . vegetables: green. . . .

1.14 . . . away, so. . . .

1.15 . . . exciting, but. . . .
. . . ability; he. . . .
. . . mystery; however, he. . . .
. . . stories: "The . . . Heart,"
. . . boring, so . . .

1.16 Example:
We had been traveling three days, so we were very glad to arrive at my aunt and uncle's house. At last Aunt Alice came to the car to welcome us. She unlocked the gate to the backyard; my dog Yipper raced around the back of the house. Suddenly we heard a loud splash and a yip, so we hurried around the house. Then we saw Yipper; he was climbing out of the swimming pool! He was really a sight: dripping wet, shaking with fear, and barking for attention.

1.17-1.20 Any order:

1.17 a. two or more adjectives preceding noun
Example:
b. The fat, ugly cat ate our hamster.

1.18 a. appositive or appositive phrase
Example:
b. The goalie, a huge Canadian, liked to crochet.

1.19 a. direct address
Example:
b. Thank you, you gracious girl, for this bouquet of daisies.

1.20 a. parenthetical expressions
Example:
b. We will, as I have said before, eat out tomorrow!

1.21 a. interrupt
b. summarize

1.22 When, Sally, do you think you're going to get the pizza?
direct address

1.23 Teflon, a non-stick coating material, is a chemical cohesion.
appositive phrase

1.24   Who, in your opinion, won the
       battle of Waterloo?
       parenthetical expression

1.25   If this car, an old junkheap, ever
       starts, we shall go!
       appositive phrase

1.26   When they heard that the "Thresher"
       was doomed, the large, hushed crowd
       moved noiselessly away.
       two adjectives before noun

1.27   Money, charm, and grace - none of
       these things will replace inner peace.
       summary statement

1.28   I think, my dear Watson, that you
       are onto something.
       direct address

1.29   Walking the tight rope, an
       amazing feat, is a dangerous career.
       appositive phrase

1.30   You are, as you well know, a
       candidate for class president.
       parenthetical expression

1.31   Birth, death, and taxes- you can't get
       away from them.
       summarizing

1.32   after an interjection
1.33   after a participial phrase
1.34   after an adverb clause
1.35-1.37 Examples:
1.35   Well, it's about time you got here.
1.36   Waiting for the wave, Jim didn't
       notice he was drifting.
1.37   Whenever I go skiing, I always
       break a pole.
1.38   . . . was brief, we decided. . .
1.39   . . . was over, Tom went. . . .
1.40   . . . like chickens, the natives. . .
1.41   Well, it wasn't. . .

1.42   . . . often risky, she wasn't. . . .

1.43   . . . the hike, the climbers. . . .

1.44   . . . to town, the people. . . .
1.45   Disgusted, we went. . .

1.46   . . . a day, the fifth. . . .

1.47   adverb clause
1.48   adverb clause
1.49   participial phrase
1.50   interjection

1.51   adverb clause
1.52   participial phrase
1.53   adverb clause
1.54   participial phrase
1.55   participial phrase
1.56   a. chastisement   n. petulant
       b. complement   o. recalcitrant
       c. confident   p. recreant
       d. covenant   q. reliant
       e. elegant   r. resilient
       f. eminent   s. significant
       g. entanglement   t. somnolent
       h. hesitant   u. subservient
       i. imminent   v. supplement
       j. impudent   w. transplant
       k. indifferent   x. variant
       l. intolerant   y. vigilant
       m. pertinent

1.57   a. noun   n. adjective
       b. noun   o. adjective
       c. adjective   p. noun, adjective
       d. noun   q. adjective
       e. adjective   r. adjective
       f. adjective   s. adjective
       g. noun   t. adjective
       h. adjective   u. adjective
       i. adjective   v. noun, verb
       j. adjective   w. noun, verb
       k. adjective   x. noun, verb
       l. adjective   y. noun, adjective
       m. adjective

1.58 Examples:
  a. Jesus took our chastisement on Himself.
  b. A predicate noun is also called a subject complement.
  c. I am confident that I am well.
  d. God made a covenant with Abraham.
  e. Her gown was quite elegant.
  f. Doctor Warren is an eminent scientist.
  g. The United States avoids entanglements with Russia.
  h. We waited because we were hesitant.
  i. The coastal hurricane was imminent.
  j. The impudent child threw his cereal bowl.
  k. He was indifferent to her pleas for mercy.
  l. Communists are intolerant of religious freedom.
  m. He gave the jury pertinent information about the murder.
  n. His petulant manner got into trouble.
  o. A recalcitrant child is an embarrassment to his parents.
  p. Martin Luther was labeled a recreant.
  q. The boy was reliant on his father's blood.
  r. Rubber is a resilient material.
  s. Science has made significant discoveries in astronomy.
  t. The somnolent village nestled in the quiet valley.
  u. John the Baptist claimed to be subservient to Jesus.
  v. Some people supplement their incomes by selling products.
  w. The kidney transplant was a total success.
  x. The blood pressure machine gives variant readings.
  y. The guards kept a vigilant watch on the tomb.

SECTION TWO

2.1 a nonfiction piece of prose literature that explains something

2.2 a formal writing which explains about some limited topic

2.3 early Romans and Greeks

2.4 essai

2.5 Any order:
  a. Bacon
  b. Steele
  c. Addison

2.6 Any order:
  a. Paine
  b. Emerson
  c. Thurber

2.7 serious

2.8 Either order:
  a. topic
  b. purpose

2.9 Any order:
  a. reasons
  b. examples
  c. incidents

2.10 inform

2.11 Pain was God's mistake. . . He should have invented a better way of alerting us.

2.12 Pain expresses the nature of our fallen world; it makes us consider other values.

2.13 woman in an accident; young man and girl on a mountain; 18 year-old athlete with cancer; grand-mother with two weeks to live; race car driver

2.14 an audible sound and a shock

2.15 The patient would switch off the signal.

2.16 It is well suited to this fallen world; it protects us from injury.

2.17 It can drive us from God. We can hate God or it can drive us to Him.

2.18 In the intensive care ward all people become one. There is no division because all are united by love; all are forced to reconsider life.

2.19 We are not abandoned. No one suffers alone because Jesus went through a life of pain.

2.20 We have hope. Jesus arose from the dead—so will we. All our hurts are temporary.

2.21 Our life is an hour of suffering compared to a lifetime of comfort—eternity.

2.22 painful, scary, and darkness

2.23 We'll be in a new world. Tears and hurts will be only memories.

2.24 Our lives are so short. Some day it will all destruct and we'll have the blessing of eternity.

2.25 teacher check

2.26 a. ize, V
b. ize, V
c. ize, V
d. ize, V
e. ize, V
f. ize, V
g. ize, V
h. ize, V
i. ize, V
j. ize, V
k. ize, V
l. ize, V
m. ize, V
n. ize, V
o. ize, V
p. yze, V
q. yze, V
r. yze, V
s. ise, V
t. ise, V
u. ise, V
v. ise, V
w. ise, V
x. ise, V
y. ise, V

2.27 vitalize

2.28 surmise

2.29 remise

2.30 sterilize

2.31 advertise

2.32 polarize

2.33 analyze

2.34 idolize

2.35 utilize

2.36 supervise

2.37 realize

2.38 dehumanize

2.39 galvanize

2.40 pulverize

2.41 energize

2.42 exercise

2.43 paralyze

2.44 characterize

2.45 patronize

2.46 mesmerize

2.47 compromise

2.48 revise

2.49 pressurize

2.50 itemize

2.51 energized, energizing

2.52 patronized, patronizing

2.53 utilized, utilizing

2.54 pulverized, pulverizing

2.55 characterized, characterizing

2.56 analyzed, analyzing

2.57 electrolyzed, electrolyzing

2.58 surmised, surmising

2.59 compromised, compromising

2.60 entertain

2.61 Either order:
a. personal/friendly
b. open/natural

2.62 humor

2.63 He has changed the situation to the opposite one.
Example:
Every dog should have a man.

2.64 Everyone should own a dog.

2.65 patience

2.66 sound teeth, gums, coat, self confidence

2.67 9, 10, and 14

2.68 don't use force, go slowly, use rewards, teach heeling, teach to retrieve, good diet, companions

2.69 Not every dog will be successful, but with patience the dog will improve.

2.70 informal

2.71 incidents

2.72 the first sentence

2.73 a. Rothschild incident (36, 37)
b. $50 incident (39, 40)
c. steps into safe (45)
d. $56 incident (65)
e. laughter when he leaves (86-88)

2.74 true

2.75 false, a manager

2.76 true

2.77 false, checking

2.78 false, fifty-six

2.79 false, laughed

2.80 false, accountant

2.81 false, morning

2.82 teacher check

2.83 a. reliable
b. excusable
c. noticeable
d. amiable
e. reprehensible
f. accessible
g. edible
h. unstable
i. profitable
j. divisible
k. attachable
l. permissible
m. probable
n. despicable
o. inevitable
p. responsible
q. lovable
r. infallible
s. eligible
t. sensible
u. unmatchable
v. collapsible
w. defensible
x. incredible
y. durable

2.84 Examples:
a. She is an amiable child.
b. The fall of Satan is inevitable.
c. God's word has proven to be infallible.
d. The fortified city was easily defensible.
e. All of the fruit of Eden was edible.

f. A true Christian is always noticeable.

g. The dam was made to be durable.
h. The unmatchable love of God is demonstrated through Jesus.
i. God is accessible through our High Priest, Jesus.
j. Her high grades in math were incredible.

SECTION ONE

1.1 Example:
Thorndike-Barnhard Advanced
Dictionary

1.2 Example:
Scott, Foresman and Company

1.3 yes or no

1.4 Example:
first page after front cover; also at
bottom of each page of dictionary

1.5 Example:
yes

1.6 Example:
21

1.7 in alphabetical order

1.8 Example:
Several ways in which I might help
myself acquire the "dictionary
habit" include always looking up
new words when I find them in my
reading, writing down new words
and their definitions, and using the
new words in sentences.

1.9 adapt

1.10 accommodate

1.11-1.12 Examples:

1.11 I tried to adapt to the cold weather.

1.12 The room must be rearranged to
accommodate our overnight guests.

1.13-1.14 Examples:

1.13 a. employer
b. responsibility
c. preparing

1.14 a. foolish
b. repair
c. old
d. automobile
e. difficulty

1.15 Examples:
a. A definition gives the exact meaning
of a word. It explains, or makes clear,
the meaning of a word.

b. A synonym describes a word gives a
shade of difference. A synonym
means the same or nearly the same
as the other word.

1.16 accommodate, 26.12

1.17 conform, 82.3

1.18 modify, 139.6

1.19 orient, 289.12

1.20 music, 461. 47

1.21 accustom, 640.10

1.22 fit, 718.8

1.23-1.25 Examples:

1.23 adoration, devotion, homage

1.24 believer, convert, disciple

1.25 Holy Writ, Scripture, the Word of God

1.26 Example:
The first version of the letter sounds
as if it had been written by someone
with a limited vocabulary. Sarah has
over-used the word nice. The second
paragraph uses synonyms such
as enjoyable, delightful, and pleasant
instead of repeating the same word.
I especially prefer spirited to nice as
a description of Sarah's horse.

1.27 a. obedient
b. hinder
c. dry
d. agreeable
e. area

1.28 e

1.29 g

1.30 c

1.31 h

1.32 f

1.33 a

1.34 i

1.35 j

1.36 b

1.37 d

1.38 death

1.39 finite

1.40 right

1.41 rebellion

1.42 bondage

1.43 weak

1.44 hate

1.45 awkward

1.46 friendly

1.47 afraid

1.48 love

1.49 active

1.50 righteousness, deceit
or truth, false

1.51 just, wicked

1.52 diligent, slothful

1.53 a. righteous
b. wicked

1.54 a. sluggard
b. diligent

1.55 a. righteous
b. wicked

1.56 a. rich
b. poor

1.57 Did you ever blink your eye?

1.58 Did you ever talk to your uncle and aunt?

1.59 Did you ever smell a scent?

1.60-1.62 Example:

1.60 I ate my breakfast at eight o'clock in the morning.

1.61 My father will sow the seeds and my mother will sew our clothing.

1.62 Do not break the wrench when you fix the car brake.

1.63 feat

1.64 fir

1.65 gait

1.66 gilt

1.67-1.76 Examples:

1.67 John split a cord of wood one day.
or The cord broke when we tried the package.

1.68 The organist struck a chord and the choir began to sing.

1.69 In the early days of our country, sealing wax was used to seal letters.

1.70 They plastered the ceiling before they laid the carpet.

1.71 "Let him that stole steal no more."

1.72 A million dollars worth of steel was used in the skeleton of the building.

1.73 "But the dove found no rest for the sole of her foot, and she returned unto him into the ark."
Genesis 8:9

1.74 "Thou shalt love the Lord thy God with all thy heart, and with all thy soul . . . and thy neighbor as thyself." Luke 10:27

1.75 The rain prevented them from going to the picnic.

1.76 The queen will reign until her death.

1.77 teacher check

1.78 Hint:
If you did not follow directions, restudy the seven suggestions for following directions.

1.79 teacher check

1.80 teacher check

1.81

```
A X P S A L M I S T D H G S T U
A B X D O C I L E D P O Z A U O
C Q B W V U N I T Y L M B L M B
C J D R B X P N F O L O Y V Z E
O X Z P E W A I S L E N O A S D
M D B Z X V C P X W X Y G T G I
M V R A Z E I P L U M M Z I P E
O J S T P S Q A B N A N Q O M N
D P A R I D K I T R X T I N K T
A F O E P X U E Y I J H O L Y X
T I N F I N I T E P O X I S L E
E T H E S A U R U S X N U C E T
```

1.82 abbreviate

1.83 saturate

1.84 communicate

1.85 abbreviation

1.86 accommodate

1.87 aisle
Example:
a passage between rows of seats

1.88 antonym

1.89 arid

1.90 communication
Example:
a giving of information by talking, writing, and so on

1.91 congenial

1.92 conservation

1.93 deceit
Example:
making a person believe as true something that is false

1.94 dexterous

1.95 docile

1.96 holy
Example:
belonging to God

1.97 homonym

1.98 infiltrate

1.99 infinite
Example:
without limits or bounds

1.100 isle

1.101 obedient

1.102 orient
Example:
to get in the right relations to the things or persons about one

1.103 psalmist

1.104 raze

1.105 salvation
Example:
deliverance from sin and from punishment for sin

1.106 saturation

1.107 slothful

1.108 sluggard
Example:
a lazy, idle person

1.109 synonym
1.110 thesaurus
1.111 undaunted
Example:
not afraid; not dismayed or
discouraged

1.112 unity
1.113 unyielding
1.114 wholly
Example:
in its entirety; in full

SECTION TWO

2.1-2.5 Examples:
2.1   drä′ mu or dra′ m ə
or
dram′ u or dram′ə
2.2   ad vur tiz munt or mənt
or
ad vėr′ tis munt or mənt
or
ad vėr′ tīz munt or mənt
2.3   bō kā
or
bü kā;
2.4   en′ vul lōp
or
en′ v əlōp
or
än′ vu lōp
or
än′ v ə lōp
2.5   u dult′ or ə dəlt
or
ad′ ult or ad′ əlt

2.6   by respelling and by diacritical
marks (markings)
2.7   at the bottom of the page and at
the beginning of the dictionary

2.8   Examples:
a. mā′ kron
b. mak′ ron
c. mā′ krun
d. mak′ run

2.9   āviātion
2.10   fāte
2.11   māde
2.12   lāte

2.13   bō kā

2.14   strĭkt lē

2.15   hĭt

2.16   ī dē u

2.17   bŏt l

2.18   cãre

2.19   môrning

2.20   cär

2.21   c

2.22   a

2.23   b

2.24   d

2.25   teacher check

2.26   verb

2.27   noun
2.28   a. reb′ el
b. ri bel′

2.29-2.32 Examples:
2.29   a. What is your favorite sub′ ject?
b. Do not sub ject′ anyone to ridicule.
2.30   a. I expect an in′ crease in salary next
month.
b. I shall try to in crease′ my savings
account.

143

2.31 a. No pro' test was expected over the decision of the judge.

      b. The heirs did not protest' the will.

2.32 a. The con' flict was over the umpire's decision.

      b. My working hours do not con flict' with church attendance.

2.33 teacher check

SECTION THREE

3.1 Example:
Because the second letter is written in standard English and sounds more mature then the first.

3.2 May I go to the library?

3.3 Mary did well on her test.

3.4 Let your sister be.
or
Leave your sister alone.

3.5 Sit down: I have something to tell you.

3.6 sunk; The boat sank in the lake during the storm.

3.7 growed; My brother has grown a beard.

3.8 sang; The choir has sung that hymn several times before.

3.9 run; John ran faster than his brother in the last race.

3.10 don't; Irene doesn't have a driver's license yet.

3.11 Him; He and I will work together on that project.

3.12 quiet; Speak quietly in the library in order not to disturb others.

3.13 couldn't find no; I couldn't find a basketball in the closet.

3.14 drunk; After the ball game, I drank a whole quart of milk.

3.15 shrunk; My new sweater shrank the last time it was washed.

3.16 sit

3.17 affect

3.18 all right

3.19 effect

3.20 set

3.21 ought to

3.22 well

3.23 taught

3.24 any

3.25 did

3.26 a. vitality
      b. vital

3.27 a. serenity
      b. serene

3.28 a. tranquility
      b. tranquil

3.29 a. responsibility
      b. responsible

3.30 a. purity
      b. pure

3.31 a. maturity
      b. mature

3.32 a. humility
      b. humble

3.33 a. spirituality
      b. spiritual

3.34 Examples:
authority, reality, community, immensity, electricity, humanity, morality, vicinity, university, hospitality

SECTION ONE

1.1 princess's

1.2 Kerry's

1.3 soldier's

1.4 shepherd's

1.5 Mr. Dicken's

1.6 boy's

1.7 man's

1.8 child's

1.9 Jones'

1.10 lady's

1.11 deer's

1.12 women's

1.13 policemen's

1.14 oxen's

1.15 salesmen's

1.16 boxes'

1.17 toys'

1.18 wives'

1.19 sopranos'

1.20 empresses'

1.21 brother-in-law's

1.22 Addison and Steele's

1.23 Esther and Eric's

1.24 Gary and Peg's

1.25 Bill of Rights'

1.26 don't

1.27 shouldn't

1.28 can't

1.29 we're

1.30 he'll

1.31 I'll

1.32 they'll

1.33 I've

1.34 it's

1.35 doesn't

1.36 forty-nine

1.37 seventy-eight

1.38 sixty-three

1.39 eighty-one

1.40 fifty-five

1.41 1732-1799

1.42 1757-1827

1.43 1867-1934

1.44 1884-1972

1.45 1917-1963

1.46 lit-er-a-ture

1.47 ex-cep-tion

1.48 sec-re-tar-y

1.49 math-e-mat-ics

1.50 tem-per-a-ture

1.51 down-in-the-mouth

1.52 an eight-year-old girl

1.53 law-school facilities

1.54 cradle-to-grave needs

1.55 double-parked automobiles

1.56 good-looking; all-important

1.57 self-satisfaction; twenty-five

1.58 vice-executive; pinstriped; light-gray

1.59 One-third; school day; unimportant
1.60 workingman; fish and chips
1.61 "I had hoped," Bill said, "that I could play Captain Courageous in the play."

1.62 "Bill," James said, "It's really you!"

1.63 Jane enjoyed reading the story "Yarn of Nancy Bell."
1.64 Chapter twelve is called "How to Pass Junior High School."

1.65 "Do you like," asked Sandra, "to read fiction or nonfiction?"

1.66 Who said "Blondes have more fun"?
1.67 teacher check
1.68 If you don't start studying more (I mean this) you will fail sixth grade.

1.69 I wore a rose corsage (I prefer roses to carnations) to the banquet.
1.70 We need (1) food, (2) shelter, and (3) clothing.

1.71 I left for college when I was eighteen (that was also the age I was married).

1.72 David Copperfield

1.73 Woman's Day
1.74 New York Journal
1.75 Pinta
1.76 Air Force One
1.77 Yesterday Dr. S. Brooks saw a picture of Queen Elizabeth.
1.78 Mr. and Mrs. Hunt were members of the Broadway Baptist Church of Topeka, Kansas.
1.79 The Steele and Wagner Company built its factory near the Mississippi River.
1.80 Have you ever read Ten Men Who Dared?

1.81 Thomas Jefferson formulated the Constitution of the United States of America.

1.82 On Friday, May 3, we will see a film on the Civil War.

1.83 Cameo soap leaves your skin silky smooth.

1.84 Many people of India believe in Buddha.
1.85 Example:
WASHINGTON - Jerry Swift turned down the final offer made by the Washington Warriors.

"If the team owners don't want me enough to pay me decently, I'll talk to another team that does!" Swift said Thursday.

The Twenty-nine-year-old star says he'll go through the draft as a free agent.

Example:
The local chapter of the Daughters of the American Revolution met Tuesday, October 30, in the Business and Professional Women's Hall. Olivia Dexter spoke about the role of women in the Revolutionary War. Her new book, Carrie of Concord, presents an unusual view of American life in the 1800s.

1.86 P.M.

1.87 Mr.

1.88 Miss.

1.89 no.

1.90 lb.

1.91 S.O.S.

1.92 oz.

1.93 Dr.

1.94 ave. or Ave.

1.95 supt. or Supt.

1.96 P.O.

1.97 mt.

1.98 Pres.

1.99 sec.

1.100 treas.

1.101 Rev.

1.102 pl.

1.103 blvd.

1.104 sr. or Sr.

1.105 jr. or Jr.

1.106 C.O.D.

1.107 gov. or Gov.

1.108 gen. or Gen.

1.109 M.D.

1.110 R.R.

1.111 Example:
8722 Main St.

1.112 Example:
Central City, Ohio 55555

1.113 Example:
July 13, 1966

1.114 Example:
LA 805 p. 15

1.115 Example:
Mon. (Monday) 3 P.M.

1.116 a. abbreviation
b. apostrophe
c. capitalization
d. contraction
e. cradle-to-grave
f. dialectal
g. down-in-the-mouth
h. hyphen
i. incidental
j. inclusive
k. italics
l. miscellaneous
m. objective
n. parentheses
o. plural
p. possessive
q. pre-existent
r. preference
s. prefix
t. President-elect
u. quotation marks
v. quoted
w. restaurant
x. ridiculous
y. self-satisfaction
z. semi-independent
aa. singular
bb. suffix
cc. syllable
dd. ultra-articulate

1.117 a. (suffix) hyphen
b. (singular) plural
c. (contraction) abbreviation
d. (italics) quotation marks
e. (prefix) syllable

1.118 Definitions are examples:
a. cradle-to-grave—from birth to death
b. down-in-the-mouth—unhappy
c. pre-existent—existing before
d. President-elect—a person who has been elected president but has not yet begun to take office
e. self-satisfaction—satisfied with oneself
f. semi-independent—partially independent
g. ultra-articulate—extremely articulate

SECTION TWO

2.1 Example:
Let your words be pure, your
message be of good report

2.2 Example:
Always speak graciously so you can
be able to speak properly and
appropriately any place to any person.

2.3 Example:
Do not use harmful words, but only
helpful words, the kind that build up
and provide what is needed, so that
what you say will do good to those
who hear you.

2.4 Example:
An idea that is well expressed is like
a design of gold, set in silver.

2.5 Example:
The words of a wise man brings him
honor, but a fool is destroyed by his
own words.

2.6 teacher check

2.7 Examples:
a. probably my pet or my hobby
b. because the other subjects are not
usually well known enough to
speak about.
c. you would have nothing to say;
little or no knowledge about the
subject.

2.8 a. strong and distinct, full of life
Example:
b. My brother leaped over the fence,
tore around the corner, and
snatched his prized baseball glove
from the mouth of the playful
puppy.

2.9 a. making a picture for the mind
Example:
b. The little stone cottage with a
thatched roof was nestled snugly
at the foot of a small hill among
the flowering dogwood and
crabapple trees.

2.10 a. figures of speech stating a likeness
between things using the words like
or as
Example:
b. The summer clouds were like fluffy
balls of cotton.

2.11 a. figures of speech in which a word that
ordinarily means one thing is applied
to another suggesting likeness
between the two
Example:
b. The clouds, fluffy cotton floated lazily
across the summer sky.

2.12 a. Figure of speech in which a lifeless
thing or quality is spoken of as if alive.
Example:
b. The moon smiled serenely upon the
sleeping village while sleepy stars
winked their approval.

2.13 Examples:
a. audience would be bored
b. more interested
c. audience might be irritated or
amused by the ridiculous antics.

2.14 3 2 1 2 2 3 1
George didn't do his homework.
(accusingly)

2.15 2 3 2 3 4
Is that really you? (surprise)

2.16 4 3 4 3
Help! I'm falling. (fear)

2.17 3 2 2 4
Please put that down.
(command)

2.18 teacher check

2.19 teacher check

2.20 teacher check

2.21 ar-tic-u-la-tion

2.22 an-i-ma-tion

2.23   char-ac-ter-i-za-tion

2.24   com-mu-ni-ca-tion

2.25   di-a-phragm

2.26   dic-tion

2.27   e-nun-ci-a-tion

2.28   ges-ture

2.29   hu-mor-ous

2.30   in-flec-tion

2.31   in-ter-pre-ta-tion

2.32   in-tro-duc-tor-y

2.33   met-a-phor

2.34   mod-u-lat-ed

2.35   mon-o-tone

2.36   pace

2.37   per-son-i-fi-ca-tion

2.38   poise

2.39   pos-ture

2.40   pro-nun-ci-a-tion

2.41   rap-port

2.42   sim-i-le

2.43   var-i-a-tion

2.44   vi-car-i-ous-ly

2.45   vol-ume

2.46   Example:
Good <u>articulation</u> commands the listener's attention.

2.47   Example:
The motorized model shows <u>animation</u>.

2.48   Example:
The actor read the <u>characterization</u> of the man and the child from the script.

2.49   Example:
Start the day with <u>communication</u> with God.

2.50   Example:
Placing his hands on his <u>diaphragm,</u> Carl felt it expand as he inhaled.

2.51   Example:
Mary's <u>diction</u> would improve if she stopped using slang.

2.52   Example:
Everyone understood, since her <u>enunciation</u> was perfect.

2.53   Example:
He made a <u>gesture</u> indicating that I should be still.

2.54   Example:
The <u>humorous</u> stories kept the people roaring with laughter.

2.55   Example:
The <u>inflection</u> of her voice changed when she became angry.

2.56   Example:
No prophecy of the Scripture is of private <u>interpretation</u>.

2.57   Example:
After a few <u>introductory</u> remarks, the chairman introduced the speaker.

2.58   Example:
He has a heart of gold is a <u>metaphor</u>.

2.59   Example:
The singer <u>modulated</u> her voice to express the various moods of the song.

2.60   Example:
A person who speaks in a <u>monotone</u> is unable to modulate his voice.

2.61   Example:
When Keith jogs, he keeps up a fast <u>pace.</u>

2.62   Example:
He who loves well, out of a pure heart, is the <u>personification</u> of all that is good.

2.63 Example:
The Haitian, carrying a load of baskets on her head, walked with perfect <u>poise</u>.

2.64 Example:
Good <u>posture</u> helps the body to function well.

2.65 Example:
The <u>pronunciation</u> of some foreign words is difficult.

2.66 Example:
The <u>rapport</u> between the two enabled them to develop a beautiful friendship.

2.67 Example:
Her eyes were like saucers is a <u>simile</u>.

2.68 Example:
The <u>variation</u> in God's creation is breathtaking.

2.69 Example:
While June was recuperating, she experienced <u>vicariously</u> incidents from the lives of many missionaries she read about.

2.70 Example:
The Bible is composed of sixty-six books in one <u>volume</u>.

SECTION THREE

3.1 <u>Across</u>
3. hear
5. sum
6. real
7. sew
8. ant
10. tail
13. seen
15. stake
16. fair
17. wee
19. ate
20. main
<u>Down</u>
1. break
2. mail
4. red
5. sea
7. so
9. there
11. per
12. bare
13. seam
14. hair
15. sea
18. in

3.2 g
3.3 v
3.4 a
3.5 n

3.6 q
3.7 u
3.8 p
3.9 l
3.10 h
3.11 x
3.12 j
3.13 e
3.14 a
3.15 r
3.16 d
3.17 w
3.18 c
3.19 s
3.20 k
3.21 f
3.22 i

3.23 m

3.24 b

3.25 y

3.26 o

3.27 t

3.28 l

3.29 j

3.30 c

3.31 h or d

3.32 n

3.33 x

3.34 o

3.35 v

3.36 b

3.37 s

3.38 u

3.39 a

3.40 f

3.41 m

3.42 r

3.43 g

3.44 k

3.45 q or v

3.46 i

3.47 d

3.48 p

3.49 w

3.50 e

3.51 t

3.52 accept

3.53 compliment

3.54 already

3.55 a. Except
b. all ready

3.56 a. council
b. counsel

3.57 a. effects
b. affect

3.58 condone

3.59 diary

3.60 dessert

3.61 deductive

3.62 a. illegible
b. eligible

3.63 concave

3.64 temerity

3.65 a. whether
b. principles

3.66 indignant

3.67 a. implicit
b. explicit

3.68 teacher check

3.69
a. accept
b. except
c. eligible
d. illegible
e. explicit
f. implicit
g. timidity
h. temerity
i. all together
j. altogether
k. all ready
l. already
m. principal
n. principle

3.70

Across	Down
1. convex	1. concave
3. affect	2. council
6. counsel	4. effect
8. explicit	5. formal
10. compliment	7. weather
11. implicit	9. timidity
12. complement	10. condone
13. condemn	14. former
16. whether	15. feign
17. temerity	
18. faint	

SECTION ONE

1.1	d	1.17	b
1.2	e	1.18	c
1.3	a	1.19	b
1.4	f	1.20	b
1.5	b	1.21	The Lord's Prayer or Our Father
1.6	true	1.22	4 through 8
1.7	false	1.23	Examples:

1.8   true

1.9   false

1.10   true

1.11   false

1.12   true

1.13   Any order:
- a. me
- b. he
- c. we
- d. him
- e. us
- f. his

1.14   student check

1.15
- a. father
- b. daughter
- c. day
- d. back
- e. mother
- f. man
- g. earth
- h. there
- i. who
- j. where
- k. sheep
- l. ship

1.16   a

1.23   Examples:
father (fæder)
will (willa)
guilt (gyltas)
our (ure)
earth (eorðan)
evil (yfele)
thou or you (þu)
art (eart)
us
to
heaven (heofonum)
day (d eg)
thine (þin)
and
name (nama)
forgive (forgyf)

1.24   Examples:
and
earth   (eorðan)
he
thorns (þornas)
some   (sum)
that   (þaet)
fell   (feoll)
good   (god)
way   (weg)
land

1.25   c

1.26   e

1.27   b

1.28   f

1.29   d

1.30   teacher check

1.31   teacher check

1.32   French

1.33   common people

1.34   failure

1.35   a. grew
        b. declined

1.36   Examples:
        A, knight (knyght), there (ther),
        was, and, that, a worthy, man,
        from (fro), the, time (tyme), he,
        first, began (bigan), To, ride,
        out, loved, chivalry (chivalrie),
        truth (trouthe), honor (honour),
        freedom (fredom), courtesy (curtesie)

1.37   Examples:
        a. Modern English i Middle English
            y—knyght and tyme
        b. final letter dropped in Middle
            English—from, there, fre,
            (freedom)
        c. The ou used in Middle English
            trouthe and honour spelled u
            or o in Modern English; ur in
            curtesie spelled ou in Modern
            English; ie in curtesie spelled
            y in Modern English

1.38   false

1.39   false

1.40   true

1.41   true

1.42   true

1.43   b

1.44   a

1.45   a

1.46   teacher check

1.47   Any order:
        a. accept
        b. remember
        c. ally
        d. attend
        e. persevere
        f. grieve
        g. repent
        h. resemble
        i. resist
        j. avenge
        k. vigil

1.48   Examples:
        a. The army is our defense.
        b. The trip was a great expense.
        c. The steam began to condense.
        d. The pain was intense.
        e. That story is nonsense.
        f. The ocean is immense.

1.49   a. condolence
        b. conference
        c. existence
        d. experience
        e. intelligence
        f. interference
        g. occurrence
        h. superintendence

SECTION TWO

2.1   Any order:
       a. and
       b. but
       c. for
       d. or
       e. nor
       f. so
       g. yet

2.2   a. the process of combining similar
           words, phrases, or clauses by
           creating pairs or a series
       b. a sentence consisting of two or
           more independent clauses

2.3-2.11 Examples:

2.3 Joe and Mary like skydiving.

2.4 I'll go to the Rockies, but I'm afraid of heights.

2.5 The last day of school is really hectic, yet that is the day most students like best.

2.6 I'll have to take the bus, for I won't fly.

2.7 Neither the antique couch nor the new dishwasher will fit in Aunt Martha's trailer.

2.8 That child can't go to school alone, so I guess I'll have to take him.

2.9 You can go to the college your sister attended or you can choose a different college.

2.10 I enjoy eating fried chicken, steak, and french fries, but my favorite food is lobster.

2.11 The United States and the United Kingdom joined the coalition, but France would have nothing to do with it.

2.12 Any order:
  a. both. . .and
  b. either. . .or
  c. neither. . .nor
  d. not only. . .but also
  e. whether. . .or

2.13-2.21 Examples:

2.13 Both the manager of the supermarket and the assistant manager may help the new employee.

2.14 Neither the minister nor the deacons will attend the meeting.

2.15 This award is given both to junior high and senior high students.

2.16 Both the Junior Varsity and the Varsity teams are riding the bus to the play-off.

2.17 Whether or not you go with us depends on your parents. (Whether you go. . . or not. . .)

2.18 Either help light the fire or go help your brother collect wood.

2.19 Not only was our kitten affected by the new water, but also our German Shepherd.

2.20 Whether we go sailing this Saturday or not depends on the weather.

2.21 Not only Jerry, but also his sister, Karen, enjoyed their trip through Italy.

2.22 Examples; Any order:
  a. also
  b. furthermore
  c. nevertheless
  d. still
  e. then
  f. therefore
  g. however
  h. moreover

2.23-2.32 Examples:

2.23 The flowers on the altar were given to the church too late for the morning service; instead, we'll use them in the evening service.

2.24 They wanted to go to New England this summer; therefore, they've saved for a whole year.

2.25 He had a firm grip of the child's hand; consequently, she did not get lost in the crowd.

2.26 We were going to try to find the rest of the party; however, no one seems to know which way they went.

2.27 The nerve endings seem to be dead; nevertheless, the doctors will have to anesthetize the patient.

2.28 The steaks in that restaurant are really tough; moreover, the vegetables are always cold.

2.29　The kite was hopelessly
　　　tangled in the tree✱; still,
　　　the little girl's father struggled
　　　to get it down.

2.30　Early Christians were persecuted
　　　for their beliefs; likewise, we may
　　　be unpopular with certain friends
　　　for His sake.

2.31　The Christian life can be exciting;
　　　besides, it can be quite fulfilling.

2.32　One commandment is to love the Lord
　　　completely; hence, we have
　　　a life-time task before us.

2.33　Examples: Any order
　　　a.　after
　　　b.　although
　　　c.　because
　　　d.　before
　　　e.　since
　　　f.　than
　　　g.　though
　　　h.　until
　　　i.　when
　　　j.　where

2.34-2.43　Examples:
2.34　You obviously like cake since you
　　　never miss a sale at the bakery!

2.35　Because Gerry hates boating, take
　　　her to the marina café, and we'll
　　　use the boat.

2.36　The church needs more money so
　　　that it can continue to support
　　　missionaries.

2.37　Dad told me I could have all my
　　　privileges when I am ready to accept
　　　the responsibility of being a man.

2.38　As long as we ignore the simple
　　　truths of the Bible, we will suffer
　　　greatly as a nation.

2.39　I don't get to sleep in my own room
　　　whenever my great Aunt Sally visits
　　　us.

2.40　After the thunderstorm is
　　　over, we go out and gather the
　　　rain water that has accumulated
　　　in the vats.

2.41　Although I seem to
　　　work on homework more
　　　than ever, I don't really
　　　mind most of it.

2.42　The highway ran right through the old
　　　park so that it wouldn't have to
　　　circle for five miles out of its way.

2.43　They wanted us to go surfing with
　　　them, as if we were experts!

2.44-2.53　Examples:
2.44　which is always on time
2.45　who is very dedicated
2.46　who came from Ohio
2.47　who is Arnold Dolby's brother
2.48　that resembles a camel
2.49　which is very expensive
2.50　that comes once a week
2.51　who was surprised by the professional
　　　performance
2.52　which were torn and musty
2.53　who lives down the block
2.54　N
2.55　R
2.56　R
2.57　N
2.58　R

2.59-2.62　Examples:
2.59　Near the cave we came across bear
　　　cubs, growling for food.

2.60　The car, an antique, uses ten to
　　　fifteen gallons of gasoline for a two-
　　　hundred-mile trip.

2.61　The church picnic, a feast, held on
　　　Thanksgiving attracted many teens,
　　　mostly our age.

✱ The correct answer, *The kite was
hopelessly tangled in the tree…* may or
may not be reflected in your version of
the LIFEPAC.

2.62　In a restaurant on the turnpike, I met a person from my home town who had been my grand-father's doctor.

2.63　A

2.64　P

2.65　P

2.66　A

2.67　A

2.68　h

2.69　e

2.70　b

2.71　a

2.72　j

2.73　f

2.74　i

2.75　c

2.76　d

2.77　g

2.78　bė r glu rē

2.79　breth ren

2.80　fôr mu lē

2.81　gov ėrn ment

2.82　ir rev u runt

2.83　līt ning

2.84　lab ru tôr ē

2.85　per fôrm

2.86　präb lē or ˋpräb (ə) ble

2.87　traj u dē

2.88　tentative

2.89　amiable

2.90　suffrage

2.91　momentous

2.92　burglary

2.93　government

2.94 – 2.105 Examples:

2.94　Jerry was the mathematician of his class.

2.95　You will undoubtedly have to go to the dentist.

2.96　The surprise party was a great success.

2.97　The flood proved to be disastrous to the community.

2.98　Everyone should be athletic for health reasons.

2.99　The old tree was split by lightning.

2.100　The mischievous child was punished.

2.101　She was formerly a reporter.

2.102　They were formally introduced.

2.103　That behavior was considered irreverent.

2.104　The fact is irrelevant to your argument.

2.105　He was granted tentative approval.

SECTION THREE

3.1 An autobiography is a narrative or story a person writes about his own life.

3.2 a. may affect author's actions and reactions or the actual writing of book
b. may affect the author and his reactions; may be the reason he or she wrote the book
c. may allow the reader to discover the real personality of the author
d. Certain events or situations may have changed the author's life.
e. A truth about life expressed by the author may influence the reader's ideas and reactions.

3.3 Either order:
a. Lonesome Valley (a rural setting)
b. early 1900s

3.4 The schoolhouse is one room. All children grades 1 through 8 study together. Many of the children must help with seasonal farm work.

3.5 no

3.6 Examples; Any order:
a. notices the needs of the children
b. takes pride in his work
c. is willing to fight for his beliefs
d. accepts the children for themselves

3.7 the fight with Guy Hawkins, which Stuart won

3.8 Hawkins respects Stuart and becomes a "real pupil," instead of a disruptive force.

3.9 Sometimes your choices may force you into unpleasant or challenging situations.

3.10-3.20 Examples; (sentences only):

3.10 a. noun
b. The tenor of the note was threatening.

3.11 a. adjective
b. The taffy was elongated as they worked with it.

3.12 a. noun
b. The controversies were settled one by one.

3.13 a. noun
b. Someone has contaminated the water in the in the cistern.

3.14 a. adverb
b. He was vaguely aware of someone in the room.

3.15 a. adverb
b. Harry reluctantly handed in his spelling paper.

3.16 a. adjective
b. The mayor is a prominent person in the town.

3.17 a. adjective
b. Some metal trash cans are galvanized.

3.18 a. noun
b. A regular census was very common in the early 1900s.

3.19 a. noun
b. The elderly woman's subsistence was meager.

3.20 a. noun
b. The recitation of his poem lasted twenty minutes

3.21 Thanksgiving Day, November 28.

3.22 an airplane in the region around the South Pole

3.23 a profusion of gear (supplies and equipment)

3.24 He is confident and competent.

3.25 He had to shout and gesture to be heard because of the engine noise.

3.26 There is a hint of a dangerous flight. It foreshadows possible trouble.

3.27 They are daring and not afraid of death.

3.28 the amount of gasoline, the weight of the plane, and the height of the pass

3.29 He is unaffected by problems. He seems to be a competent person.

3.30 He is selfless and dedicated.

3.31 They hit rough air. They weren't gaining altitude fast enough and had to throw out food.

3.32 Byrd knows these men and their devotion to their objectives. He can make a decision under stress.

3.33 They rise above the "Hump" safely in paragraphs 43 and 44.

3.34 He was very brave. He takes none of the glory and remembers a dead friend.

3.35 Don't give up; you can do anything if you have will power.

3.36 e

3.37 l

3.38 i

3.39 m

3.40 f

3.41 k

3.42 n

3.43 b

3.44 a

3.45 h

3.46 g
3.47 d

3.48 j

3.49 o

3.50 c
3.51 p

3.52 teacher check

3.53-3.60 Examples:

3.53 I enjoy reading a personal narrative.

3.54 That information is irrelevant.

3.55 He took scrupulous care of the expensive automobile.

3.56 They climbed the precipitous terrain.

3.57 The volcano was conical in shape.

3.58 A profusion of blooms covered the bushes.

3.59 Humans must be aware of their fallibility.

3.60 His visage was one of gloom.

3.61 <u>Across</u>
2. fallibility
3. consternation
4. eminence
5. precipitous
6. oscillations
7. visage
8. sedulously
<u>Down</u>
1. maligned
3. conical
5. profusion

SECTION ONE

1.1   something other than its
        primary meaning

1.2   those that promote advertising
        and politics

1.3   misleading

1.4   evaluate them

1.5-1.11   Examples:

1.5   MacDonald's - a break

1.6   Cross pens - prestige

1.7   Lemon - cleanliness

1.8   Lincoln - honesty

1.9   Pepsi - youth

1.10   Maytag - dependability

1.11   Rock of Gibraltar - strength

1.12   denotation

1.13   connotations

1.14   affective connotation

1.15   Examples; any order:
        a. victory (joy)
        b. tranquility (peace)
        c. faith (trust)
        d. dependable (reliable)
        e. loyal (faithful)

1.16   The reader could be easily de-
        cieved and misled by false information.

1.17   teacher check

1.18   context

1.19   clean

1.20   Example:
        All the girls ended up in the pool
        at the party.
        They had a pool party.

1.21   They were on strike. He
        will strike me.
        The board broke. He is on the board.
        Take my order now. The
        meeting is out of order.

1.22   Example:
        on your 91st birthday

1.23   directive words

1.24   R

1.25   NR

1.26   R

1.27   NR

1.28   R

1.29   Example:
        "You can't eat just one."

1.30   If any man be in Christ He is a new
        creature.

1.31   false

1.32   true

1.33   false

1.34   true

1.35   examination of all the facts

1.36   the desire to belong to certain groups

1.37   Either order:
        a. the author's bias
        b. the reader's bias

1.38   a. implied
        b. stated

1.39   facts

1.40   bias

1.41	unwarranted inference	1.67	b, e
1.42	oversimplification	1.68	t, e
1.43	ignoring alternatives	1.69	c
1.44	appeal to the emotion rather to the intellect	1.70	w, e
		1.71	u
1.45	Bias is an unbendable opinion toward someone (thing).	1.72	u, e
1.46	An unwarranted inference is an unjustifiable implication about someone (thing) negative.	1.73	th
		1.74	c or s, s
1.47	Oversimplification is stating a concise, easy answer to a difficult, complex problem.	1.75	d, e
		1.76	lo
1.48	Ignored alternatives is the presentation of usually one solution or idea, ignoring viable alternatives.	1.77	k or c, w, d, e
		1.78	n, h, e
1.49	Emotional appeal tries to elicit action by emotion rather than intellect.	1.79	g
		1.80	d, o, e
1.50	the black or white fallacy	1.81	a, s, e
1.51	to belong to a group		
1.52	bandwagon	1.82	p, e
1.53	emotional appeal	1.83	y
1.54	desired public opinion	1.84	i
1.55	true	1.85	l
1.56	false	1.86	m
1.57	true	1.87	q
1.58	false	1.88	f
1.59	c, e	1.89	a
1.60	w, l	1.90	j
1.61	n	1.91	u
1.62	p, h	1.92	r
1.63	b, s	1.93	t
1.64	c, i	1.94	h
1.65	c, b	1.95	g
1.66	n		

1.96   b
1.97   v
1.98   o

1.99   x

1.100   s
1.101   k

1.102   d

1.103   c
1.104   e
1.105   w

1.106   p
1.107 to 1.111   Examples:
1.107   My parents have no <u>mortgage</u> on their home.
1.108   The serpent in the garden was very <u>subtle</u>.
1.109   Adam and Eve <u>succumbed</u> to temptation.
1.110   The snake was forced to <u>writhe</u> on his belly.
1.111   He gave a <u>solemn</u> description of the accident.

SECTION TWO

2.1   true
2.2   false
2.3   true

2.4   false
2.5   miniature composition

2.6   so the reader can digest sections of information

2.7   the topic sentence

2.8   true
2.9   true
2.10   true

2.11   false

2.12   long paragraph
2.13   It restates and summarizes the paragraph.

2.14   narrative writing
2.15   Any Order:
     a. descriptive details
     b. important events
     c. dialogue

2.16   descriptive
2.17   expository
2.18   Either order:
     a. thorough
     b. concise or informative

2.19   Example:
<u>If one subject is abused in this country it's dieting</u>. So many false claims have been made. There just isn't any easy way to lose weight—no candies, no combination of foods, no week plans, and gadgets can substitute for keeping track of your calorie intake. Unless you eat the proper amounts of foods from the basic food groups, you will not be healthy, and you will not lose weight.

2.20   subject

2.21   organization

2.22   4
2.23   6
2.24   3

2.25   1

2.26   5

2.27   2

2.28   at the front, To the left, at the
        back, Beside the right wall, the
        rest of, The entire house, every-
        where

2.29   Some parents are more interested
        in social life.

2.30   Some parents are too involved in
        work.

2.31   Children look to outside sources
        for attention.

2.32   Children often get into
        trouble while searching for acceptance.

2.33   Parents find out too late what
        neglect has done to their children.

2.34-2.39 Examples:

2.34   Some people may choose
        to follow the crowd and go to the
        well traveled road.

2.35   Life sometimes will present problems
        and obstacles that must be overcome.

2.36   Life will present its times of
        peace and beauty.

2.37   In life we often come to places
        where important decisions will lead
        us one way or another.

2.38   Our life can often serve to guide
        another who will travel the way
        we have.

2.39   Our lives must one day end also.

2.40   true

2.41   true

2.42   false

2.43   chronological order

2.44   spatial, or particular to general

2.45   comparison/contrast

2.46   d

2.47   e

2.48   a

2.49   b

2.50   c

2.51   Example:
        Spatial order. The room was in perfect
        disarray. The dining room table was
        overturned and the chairs were scattered
        about the room. The safe on the wall
        was ripped open with the remaining
        contents hanging out. To the right a
        gaping hole attested to the intruder's
        entry, and at my feet the contents
        of the china cabinet were strewn. The
        left part of the room was untouched—
        perhaps the Christian plaque in the
        center of the wall had something
        to do with it.

2.52   woven together and flow into each other

2.53   is to bridge and unite clauses or
        sentences

2.54   a. continuity of thought
        b. pronoun reference
        c. transition words

2.55   teacher check

2.56   arctic

2.57   arraignment

2.58   auxiliary

2.59   bouquet (que = a)

2.60   circuit

2.61   eighth (ei = a)

2.62   exhausted

2.63   exhilarate

2.64   height

2.65   isthmus

2.66   lieutenant

162

2.67 pageant

2.68 parliament

2.69 receipt

2.70 rheumatism

2.71 rhyme

2.72 shepherd

2.73 sovereignty

2.74 stretched

2.75 thoroughly

2.76 twelfth

2.77 vehicle

2.78 virtue

2.79 tongue

2.80 whether (no silent letter)

2.81-2.90 Examples:

2.81 The <u>Arctic</u> is still a vastly unexplored region.

2.82 She held a faded <u>bouquet</u> in her hands.

2.83 I was the <u>eighth</u> person to pass through the door.

2.84 The passengers were <u>exhausted</u> after swimming all night.

2.85 Neither <u>height</u> nor depth can separate us from God's love.

2.86 A <u>lieutenant</u> is ranked higher than a sergeant in the service.

2.87 My grandmother's <u>rheumatism</u> keeps her awake all night.

2.88 Not all poems have to <u>rhyme.</u>

2.89 The <u>tongue</u> can be a dangerous weapon but may also be a healer.

2.90 I <u>stretched</u> my mental capabilities on that test!

2.91 isthmus

2.92 tongue

2.93 whether

2.94 shepherd

2.95 height

2.96 S

2.97 S

2.98 A

2.99 S

2.100 S

2.101 A

2.102 A

2.103 A

2.104 S

2.105 A

SECTION THREE

3.1 true

3.2 false

3.3 true

3.4 true

3.5 false

3.6 true

3.7 It introduces the subject.

3.8 Avoid opening with a biased opinion instead of a statement with which the reader can agree.

3.9 Open with general information working your way to your thesis.

3.10 Avoid catchy or clever phrases.

3.11   Example:
Books are designed to meet a reader's individual tastes and needs. Although hundreds of categories exist, few hold as much attention as the Christian novel. In a well written novel, the reader is able to participate actively and tries to evaluate the circumstances, problems, and solutions posed in the story. Novels that present true-to-life themes are the most interesting. <u>Pilgrim's Progress</u> is one of the best books I have ever read.

3.12   true
3.13   false
3.14   true
3.15   true
3.16   false
3.17   true
3.18   false
3.19   organization
3.20   Any order:
a. reasons
b. examples
c. incidents
3.21   a. to develop a strong case for your thesis
b. to research opposing views
3.22   the strongest arguments should go there—they remain in the reader's mind
3.23   proving that marathon running is very strenuous
3.24   He is using opposing or different views and is proving that he is right.
3.25   The transition phrase "most important of all."
3.26   teacher check
3.27   It summarizes the content of the paper.

3.28   It begins with a specific statement and moves to general statements.

3.29   false
3.30   true
3.31   true
3.32   true
3.33   e
3.34   h
3.35   j
3.36   i
3.37   f
3.38   b
3.39   c
3.40   k
3.41   d
3.42   a
3.43   it just lists items in the body; rewords the thesis word for word; it is sterile and unimaginative.
3.44   three things: it has variety and imagination, and it summarizes the main idea.

3.45   restate thesis with variety; develop major ideas from body with imagination; generalize at the end with a statement the reader can ponder
3.46   RO, Put a period before "He," or use a connective like "because" after he.
3.47   F, Add "Perhaps. . ." to main clause; it is a parenthetical expression.
3.48   F, Add "Just about. . . town" to the first clause, or make it a sentence, "That was just about . . ." by adding subject and verb.

3.49   F, Add "For instance . . . ago" to the first clause with a comma or make a new sentence by adding additional information to the last clause. "For instance . . . several weeks ago was the result of too much overconfidence."

3.50 RO, Make two sentences by putting a period after "high." or correct the sentence by putting a semicolon after high.

3.51 RO, Make two sentences with a period after time, or connect with conjunction "and."

3.52 S

3.53 F, Join first clause to the second to make one sentence. Change period to comma.

3.54 S

3.55 F, Make into one sentence by putting comma after "confusing" or add subject and verb to the last clause, such as "Tom also felt that none . . . fire."

3.56 teacher check

3.57 ad ver(tise)ment

3.58 a nal(y)sis

3.59 bach(e)lor

3.60 ben(e)fit ed

3.61 cal en(dar)

3.62 co(ma)

3.63 com(par)a tive

3.64 com(pe)ti tion

3.65 com(ple)ment

3.66 cor(ps)

3.67 (de) scrip tion

3.68 de sir(a)ble

3.69 dis(si) pate

3.70 ex is (tence)

3.71 Feb(ru)ar y

3.72 (for)ty

3.73 g(ua)rd

3.74 im per(a)tive

3.75 main(te)nance

3.76 min(utes)

3.77 op(por)tu ni ty

3.78 rep(e)ti tion

3.79 sep(a)rate

3.80 tor men(tor)

3.81-3.90 Examples:

3.81 sufficient, enough

3.82 examination, interpretation

3.83 been aided or helped

3.84 worthwhile, advantageous

3.85 waste, squander, vanish

3.86 occurrence, living, being

3.87 necessary, urgent

3.88 something done or said over and over

3.89 divide, set apart, to sort

3.90 one who harasses or inflicts pain

3.91 to 3.102 Examples:

3.91 The advertisement used an emotional appeal.

3.92 The bachelor lived alone on the fourth floor.

3.93 She finally awoke from the coma.

3.94 Competition drives some people to work even harder.

3.95 We studied the use of complements in grammar today.

3.96 He joined the Marine Corps right after school.

3.97 A city devotes much time to the <u>maintenance</u> of streets.

3.98 <u>February</u> is one of the coldest months in Michigan.

3.99 The <u>guard</u> was sleepy after being on duty all night.

3.100 Four times ten is <u>forty</u>.

3.101 <u>Minutes</u> sometimes seem like hours in a dentist's office.

3.102 Some <u>opportunities</u> come only once in a lifetime.

SECTION ONE

1.1 teacher check

1.2 Any order:
   a. heading
   b. inside address
   c. salutation
   d. body
   e. closing
   f. signature

1.3 a. eight lines
   b. one or two inches

1.4 a. six to ten lines
   b. one or two inches

1.5 a. two lines
   b. skip a line

1.6 a. double space
   b. skip a line (two lines)

1.7 a. two lines
   b. skip a line

1.8 a. four lines
   b. one and one-half to two inches

1.9 teacher check

1.10 teacher check

1.11 teacher check

1.12 Any order:
   a. heading
   b. salutation

   c. body
   d. closing
   e. signature

1.13 Either order:
   a. one-half inch from the top of the page
   b. on the right-hand side of the page

1.14 a comma

1.15 yes

1.16 the first word and words that refer to God

1.17 a comma

1.18 Either order:
   a. Only the first name is usually used.
   b. Your name is not printed a second time.

1.19 one-half inch

1.20 teacher check

1.21 teacher check

1.22 teacher check

1.23 teacher check

SECTION TWO

2.1   Any order:
    a. sound
    b. hearing
    c. recognition
    d. response

2.2   frequency

2.3   intensity

2.4   attention

2.5   100

2.6   Examples:
    a. the usual meaning expressed
       by the words; at face value
    b. to intend without actually
       saying; to suggest
    c. the representative, underlying,
       or symbolic meaning

2.7   facts

2.8   believable

2.9   situation

2.10 Any order:
    a. shade meanings
    b. be poetic
    c. be symbolic

2.11 literally

2.12 implying

2.13 inferring

2.14 Either order:
    a. politeness
    b. kindness

2.15 Either order:
    a. unusual use of words in the
       situation
    b. interpreting the speaker's
       remarks through a knowledge
       of his personality
    or listen for what is left unsaid

2.16 Either order:
    a. politicians
    b. advertisers

2.17 simile

2.18 metaphor

2.19 metaphor

2.20 exaggeration

2.21 irony

2.22 satire

2.23 teacher check

2.24 teacher check

2.25-2.29 Examples:

2.25 unsure or excited

2.26 excited or frightened

2.27 angry

2.28 sarcasm

2.29 softly

2.30 teacher check

2.31-2.35 Examples:

2.31 impatience

2.32 anger

2.33 disinterest or resistance, hostility

2.34 uncertainty or lying

2.35 concern/interest

2.36 Any order:
    a. understands process of listening
    b. understands literal and
       implied meanings
    c. understands use of figures of speech
    d. can interpret such nonverbal
       messages as gestures and
       expressions
    e. can interpret voice tone
    f. wants to listen attentively

2.37 teacher check

2.38 teacher check

SECTION THREE

3.1 true

3.2 false

3.3 true

3.4 true

3.5 false

3.6 true

3.7 false

3.8 teacher check

Answers may vary (3.9-3.18).

3.9 yes/no

3.10 yes/no

3.11 yes/no

3.12 yes/no

3.13 yes/no

3.14 yes/no

3.15 yes/no

3.16 yes/no

3.17 yes/no

3.18 yes/no

3.19 teacher check

3.20 teacher check

3.21 true meaning

3.22 comparison

3.23 size

3.24 question

3.25 make-up

3.26 teacher check

3.27 primary

3.28 reference

3.29 general

3.30 secondary

3.31 a. 3

b. 4

c. 1

d. 2

e. 3

f. 1

g. 2

h. 4

3.32 byline

3.33 wire service

3.34 who, what, when, where, why, and how

3.35 editorial

3.36 first amendment to the Constitution

3.37 advertising

3.38 a. editorial cartoons

b. editorial

3.39 syndicated

3.40 filler

3.41 tabulated materials

3.42 Newspapers are the only news source that gives in depth reports on current events.

3.43 Any order:

a. *Time*

b. *Newsweek*

c. *U.S. News and World Report*

3.44 *Business Week*

3.45 *Reader's Guide to Periodical Literature* or consult a computerized database

3.46 Either order:

a. microfilm

b. microfiche

3.47 teacher check

3.48 teacher check

SECTION ONE

1.1 German

1.2 French

1.3 Chaucer

1.4 Either order:
a. evangelism
b. trade

1.5 c

1.6 e

1.7 d

1.8 b

1.9 a

1.10 c

1.11 d

1.12 e

1.13 a

1.14 b

1.15 a, d, f, g, j

1.16 Examples:
a. ME, OE, OHG, L, OF, F
b. ME
c. F

1.17 a. Latin, "justus"
b. Greek "panikos," of Pan, the god who aroused terror in lonely places
c. probably Old French, from "chanter", to sing
d. from Greek, "ostreon"
e. Old English "often"
f. from French "carrousel"
g. from Greek "kalos," beautiful, plus "eidos," form, plus scope
h. from Old French, "entreferir," meaning to strike each other
i. from Hindi, "chint"
j. from Old English, "meod," meaning mead

1.18 OPTIONAL; teacher check

1.19 Examples:
a. Stringer's late ralley rips Runners, 4-1.
b. The Z-28 is a limited-edition Camaro, carefully hot-rodded by the factory with 4-barrel carb, and a high performance engine.
c. Although some older words might be combined or modified to fit certain inventions, other technical advancements used new concepts, requiring new names and expressions.

1.20 teacher check

1.21 false

1.22 true

1.23 false

1.24 false

1.25 true

1.26 a. noun
b. verb
c. verb
d. verb
e. adjective
f. noun
g. adjective
h. adverb
i. adjective
j. adverb
k. adjective
l. noun
m. noun
n. adjective
o. adjective

1.27 a. argument
      b. athlete
      c. believe
      d. benefited
      e. business
      f. fulfill
      g. government
      h. grammar

      i. height
      j. independent
      k. intelligence
      l. proceed
      m. receive
      n. repetition
      o. restaurant

SECTION TWO

2.1   We haven't been to any ball games in over a month.

2.2   Without getting an extra day, I can't see how I can finish the job.

2.3   Jim should never have gone without you.

2.4   I can't sing very well either.

2.5   I'm tired of being captain because nobody does anything.

2.6   We can hardly get along without Tom.

2.7   You haven't seen anything yet!

2.8   The time comes in a man's life when he doesn't want any help.

2.9   Unless everybody shows up, our plans don't matter.

2.10 The water is scarcely enough for the three of us.

2.11 John's ice cream fell in the mud as he was running down the street.

2.12 Looking through the library, one can find several books on horses.

2.13 Flipping through the telephone directory, he found the name he wanted.

2.14 While eating breakfast one morning, he got the idea.

2.15 Picking up his pencil, Tom noticed his shoes were untied.

2.16 To eat a tangerine, you should first remove the peel.

2.17 To be a farmer these days, a person is required to have a knowledge of chemistry.

2.18 To catch the bus on time, I would have to run five blocks.

2.19 To see clearly underwater, one must wear goggles.

2.20 To understand the history professor, you ought to read his new book.

2.21 While I am jogging, my shoelaces come untied.

2.22 If adopted, my plan, I hope, will lead to lower taxes.

2.23 When I was three, I was taught by my grandfather to play checkers.

2.24 When I am reading, my eyes grow tired.

2.25 If I were late, I would be punished by my mother.

2.26 he

2.27 one

2.28 he

2.29 a. he   b. is

2.30 a. he   b. wants

2.31 In this snowstorm nobody could find his way home.

2.32 The team has elected its new captain.

2.33 Neither Mary nor her friend wanted her picture taken.

2.34 Mary and her friend did their best to hide from the photographer.

2.35 The person who left his banana peel on my chair had better come and get it.

2.36 One needs a tractor to plow his field.

2.37 Anyone wishing to teach Sunday school should bring his Bible to church next Sunday.

2.38 Will somebody please say what he means?

2.39 I would prefer that Robert and John found their own rides home.

2.40 If the Boy Scouts work hard, they will earn merit badges.

2.41 is
2.42 is
2.43 are
2.44 Is
2.45 is
2.46 a
2.47 c
2.48 b
2.49 a

2.50 you would stop

2.51 pay

2.52 I don't want you to

2.53 started

2.54 will begin
2.55 thought

2.56 was
2.57 forgot

2.58 a. exaggerate
b. omission
c. perceive
d. parallel
e. vacuum
f. optimistic
g. usually
h. grammatical
i. unnecessary
j. dinosaurs

2.59 a. un nec es sar y
b. gram mat i cal
c. par al lel
d. ex ag ger ate
e. em bar rass
f. oc cur rence
g. oc ca sion al ly
h. nec es sar y
i. mis spelled
j. dis sat is fied
k. o mis sion
l. u su al ly

SECTION THREE

3.1 the creation of night and day, heaven and earth

3.2 the Spirit of God
3.3 the first day of Creation

3.4 Divine Power

3.5 because it was good

3.6 a statement, usually coming at the beginning of the report, indicating the direction of the report

3.7 a step-by-step examination of how something works

3.8 how the agent accomplished the action

3.9 a presentation or explanation of information, such as a travel log

3.10 What were the agent's motives? For what reason was the action done?

3.11 false

3.12 true

3.13 true

3.14 false

3.15 The president sometimes made major decisions without the consent of his advisors.

3.16 Classical music is much different from big band music.

3.17 I caught three bass at Lake Mead.

3.18 Looking back on it, I believe Thanksgiving at Grandma's place last year was the best I ever had.

3.19 The aspirin upset his stomach.

3.20 looking at the members of your audience when you speak

3.21 speaking loudly enough for everyone in the room to hear

3.22 motions of the hands or body used for emphasis while speaking

3.23 the highness or lowness of the voice

3.24 to form words carefully while speaking

3.25 teacher check

3.26 e

3.27 p

3.28 f

3.29 h

3.30 i

3.31 k

3.32 l

3.33 o

3.34 d

3.35 a

3.36 b

3.37 c

3.38 j

3.39 m

3.40 n

3.41

SECTION ONE

1.1 Example:
  a. Adam names the animals.
  b. Adam describes Eve and calls her woman.

1.2 Indo-European

1.3 true

1.4 false

1.5 true

1.6 true

1.7 false

1.8 Jesus, Bethlehem, Judea, days, Herod, king, men, east, Jerusalem, King, Jews, star, east

1.9 arose, led, began, to accuse, saying, found, perverting forbidding, to give, saying, is

1.10 a. the Bible, it
  b. the flower's, its
  c. Mary, you - Alice, me
  d. the members of the congregation, themselves

1.11 This, unusual, miraculous, many little, this, blessed, tired, weary, warm, clean, friendly, young, bright, new, special

1.12 a. reported
  b. gladly

1.13 a. looked
  b. anxiously

1.14 a. headed
  b. excitedly

1.15 a.   June 24, 1976
  Dear Jill,
  I can hardly wait to see you at camp. I'll be at Camp Inspiration on the sixteenth of this month. I hope you are as excited about this retreat as I am. Don't forget to bring your tennis racquet, swim suit, and a Bible. Last year camp was a real experience for me. The way we shared our love of Christ was as inspiring as the beautiful surroundings of the pine forest. I'll bet that's why it's called Camp Inspiration. Look for me on July 16.
                    Yours in Christ,
                    Sally Simpson

  b. Sally Simpson
    247 Norfolk Way
    Allen Town, Missouri 63001

  c. Jill Baker
    426 W. Elm Street
    Phoenix, Arizona 85007

1.16 Acronyms are letters of the abbreviated title of an organization used as words.

1.17 Numbers under 100 should be spelled out when writing a paragraph.

1.18 A period usually ends an abbreviation.

1.19 a. The Brown Co.
  b. Box 14
  c. Greenton, Ill.

1.20 a. Capt.
  b. P.O. or p.o.
  c. lb.
  d. etc.

1.21 Won't, aren't, comin'

1.22 I'm, listenin', can't

1.23 My brother-in-law served in the army (1975-1978) as a special assistant to the commander-in-chief's staff advisors. His immediate superior had been in the service for twenty-seven years. He had served under ex-President Eisenhower during World War II. My brother-in-law is now a reporter and plans one day to be editor in chief of his paper. Since he is a stick-to-it type of person he will probably succeed.

1.24 alphabetically
1.25 Any order:
   a. pronunciation
   b. definition
   c. etymology
   or spelling
1.26 Noah Webster
1.27 finding synonyms
1.28 Hint:
   a. An acceptable answer should
      include meaningful synonyms
      for major words of the Pledge
      of Allegiance. "I promise to
      support the emblem . . . ."
   b. Acceptable answers should
      include synonyms which
      paraphrase the prayer taught
      by Christ. "Our God who lives
      in celestial glory, holy is
      your title . . . ."
1.29 teacher check
1.30 I have no quarter.
   or I haven't a quarter.
1.31 We can hardly see the sky.
   or We can't see the sky.
1.32 John thought the flood, a natural
   disaster, would make a good news
   story.
1.33 When a boy reaches high school, he
   must consider the future.
1.34 John and his friend did their
   homework.
1.35 Any order:
   a. run-on
   b. fragment
   c. comma splice

1.36 Either order:
   a. subject
   b. predicate

1.37 a. F
   b. C-S
   c. RO
   d. F
   e. F

   f. C-S
   g. S
   h. C-S
   i. S
   j. S
   k. RO
1.38 teacher check
1.39 Any three in any order:
   a. topic sentence
   b. paragraph has a specific purpose
   c. paragraph is coherent
   or sentences relate to the topic
1.40 Coherence is a logical
   order for clarity in paragraphs.
1.41 Either order:
   a. chronological order
   b. spatial order
1.42 Linking expressions connect ideas and
   smooth transitions between sentences
   in paragraphs.
1.43 Any order:
   a. application
   b. adjustment
   c. order
1.44 Any order:
   a. informal or friendly
   b. invitation
   c. thank-you
1.45-1.48 Examples:
1.45 salutation or opening, "Dear John,"
1.46 ending or closing phrase, "Yours truly,"
1.47 address to a business above the
   greeting in a business letter
1.48 the message or purpose of the letter
1.49 The most difficult part is
   getting started.

1.50 a. choose a subject
   b. gather material
   c. organize thought in outline
      form
   d. expand outline to sentences
      and paragraphs
   e. write the rough draft

1.51　research
1.52　brainstorming
1.53　Hints:
　　　a.　You should have eight or ten
　　　　　ideas listed. Some of these
　　　　　words may be qualities such as
　　　　　faith, love, etc.; others may
　　　　　be examples of behavior.
　　　b.　Be sure that your outline has
　　　　　at least three main divisions
　　　　　and that each main division
　　　　　has at least two subdivisions.
　　　　　Be sure your outline has a
　　　　　logical sequence.
　　　c.　Write each outline heading as
　　　　　a topic sentence. The
　　　　　subheadings under it should be
　　　　　supporting ideas or details.
　　　　　Be sure you use complete
　　　　　sentences.
　　　d.　teacher check
　　　e.　teacher check
　　　f.　teacher check
1.54　b
1.55　b
1.56　a
1.57　a
1.58　c
1.59　b
1.60　a
1.61　e
1.62　b
1.63　e

1.64　e
1.65　teacher check
1.66　a.　kernal
　　　b.　isle, I'll
　　　c.　core
　　　d.　cord
　　　e.　sent, cent
　　　f.　rain
　　　g.　Nice, (France)
　　　h.　slay
　　　i.　wholly
　　　j.　aisle, I'll
　　　k.　raise
　　　l.　holy
　　　m.　principle
　　　n.　all ready
　　　o.　compliment
　　　p.　council
　　　q.　all together
　　　r.　racket
　　　s.　assent
　　　t.　nay
1.67　Examples:
　　　a.　I don't know whether I'll go or
　　　　　stay.
　　　b.　The weather is beautiful today.
　　　c.　Everyone except Tom is here.
　　　d.　I cannot accept such an expensive
　　　　　gift.
　　　e.　All personnel should attend the
　　　　　company meeting.
　　　f.　Those papers and letters are
　　　　　personal.
　　　g.　Lack of sunlight will affect
　　　　　plant growth.
　　　h.　The effects of radiation can be
　　　　　drastic.
1.68　teacher check

SECTION TWO

2.1　Any order:
　　　a.　gestures
　　　b.　facial expressions
　　　c.　pantomime

2.2　Examples:
　　　a.　the usual meaning of a word
　　　b.　acting without words using
　　　　　gestures and movement to tell
　　　　　a story or explain a mood

2.3　Examples:
　　　a.　fist shaking, shoulder shrugging,
　　　　　beckoning, head nodding, head
　　　　　shaking
　　　b.　moved eyebrows, widened eyes,
　　　　　moved hands
2.4　the face
2.5　eyes, eyebrows, mouth, nose

2.6   pucker, grimace, pout, smile, frown, fall open

2.7   wink, blink, flutter, stare, lower, shut, gaze

2.8   wrinkle, twitch, sniff, sneer

2.9   teacher check

2.10   Example:
        fist shaking

2.11   Example:
        pointing, fist in palm

2.12   Example:
        beckoning

2.13   Example:
        arms uplifted and spread, hands outstretched in blessing

2.14   Any order:
        a. body movements
        b. gestures
        c. facial expressions

2.15   Any order:
        a. traffic control
        b. officials for sports events
        c. sign language for the deaf
        d. making daily speech more
           expressive

2.16   teacher check

2.17   true

2.18   true

2.19   false

2.20   false

2.21   Any order:
        a. to inform
        b. to persuade
        c. to entertain

2.22   Either order:
        a. logical
        b. clear

2.23   Any order:
        a. gestures
        b. facial expressions
        c. posture

2.24   Examples:
        a. comfortingly (Matthew 9:23)
        b. commandingly (Matthew 10:5)
        c. ". . . Jesus straitly charged
            them . . . ." (Matthew 9:30)

2.25   teacher check

2.26   Any order:
        a. what action - what?
        b. what agent - who?
        c. what setting - where? and when?
        d. what means - how?
        e. what purpose - why?

2.27   Example:
        Alice, Mary Worthington called.
        She will pick you up twenty minutes
        early for choir practice. Please
        be ready.

2.28   a. Alice
        b. Mary Worthington
        c. Mary picking up Alice for choir
            practice early

2.29

2.30   a. $3\frac{1}{2}''$ X $3\frac{1}{2}''$
        b. a cross

2.31   a. acknowledge
        b. annihilate
        c. burglary
        d. calendar
        e. Christianity

f. conference
g. deceit
h. guarantee
i. imperative
j. interrupt
k. involuntary
l. irrelevant
m. kidnaped
n. laboratory
o. omitting
p. opportunity
q. picnicker
r. prerogative
s. recurring
t. reference
u. restaurant
v. separate
w. tentative
x. thoroughly
y. Wednesday
2.32 a. accessible
b. infallible
c. permissible
d. responsible

2.33 a. amiable
b. desirable
c. excusable
d. lovable
e. unstable
2.34 a. confident
b. efficient
c. obedient
d. pertinent
e. pre-existent
f. somnolent
g. supplement
2.35 a. covenant
b. elegant
c. extravagant
d. hesitant
e. irrelevant
f. lieutenant
g. significant
h. unpleasant
i. vigilant
2.36 teacher check

SECTION THREE

3.1 a. <u>u</u>nnecessary
b. <u>in</u>complete
c. <u>pre</u>test
d. <u>dis</u>believe
e. hope<u>less</u> <u>ness</u>
f. re<u>jection</u>
g. bapt<u>ism</u>
h. <u>pre</u>cious
i. <u>dis</u>courage
j. athle<u>tic</u>
k. Chris<u>tian</u>
l. life<u>like</u>
m. silli<u>ness</u>
n. beauti<u>ful</u>
o. <u>under</u>coat<u>ing</u>
3.2 a. <u>holi</u>ness, holy
b. <u>dep</u>th, deep
c. <u>mira</u>culous, miracle
d. <u>sens</u>ible, sense
e. <u>happi</u>ness, happy

3.3 Examples:
a. loving or loved

b. insight
c. reasoned or reasoning
d. disown
e. contentment
f. repeated or repeating
g. unglued
h. helpless, helped, or helping
i. sifted or presift
j. biannual
k. psalmist
3.4 A morpheme is the smallest meaningful word unit in the English language.
3.5 a. noun
b. rain
3.6 a. verb
b. climbed or jumped
3.7 a. adjective
b. gloomy
3.8 anxious, pleading
3.9 unbeatable
3.10 payment
3.11 harmful

3.12 a. infant
b. toddler
c. teen-ager
d. father
e. grandpa

3.13 a. Matthew
b. Mark
c. Luke
d. John
e. Acts

3.14 a. decide to have a party
b. set the date
c. make a guest list
d. stamp the invitations
e. mail the invitations

3.15 a. F
b. F
c. O
d. F
e. O

3.16 teacher check

3.17 a. Any order:
who, what, where, when
b. yes
c. that Mrs. Eldea Taylor from California attended her granddaughter's wedding

3.18 Examples:
a. Jimmy Carter
b. The White House, Washington, D.C.
c. Saturday, January 12, 1977
d. He explained his Christian beliefs.
e. He was interviewed by a reporter.
f. Hint:
Most of the answers will appear in the first paragraph of the story.

3.19 Examples:
a. Bethesda Mayor's wife has quintuplets in Norfolk, Virginia, Saturday.
b. Children's Home will benefit from the picnic at Jay's Barn on Saturday, May 5.

3.20 a. yes
b. yes

3.21 a. It is factual. It attempts to explain rather than to entertain.

b. Example:
Pain makes the Christian aware of a morally fallen world.

3.22 a. Example:
serious topic in the first one; the formal essay is logical and clearly organized; the informal essay attempts to be humorous; the formal essay tries to provide information and prove an opinion
b. formal
c. informal

3.23 teacher check

3.24 a. acquire
b. solemn
c. psychology
d. indebtedness
e. mortgage
f. guarantee
g. scissors
h. disguise
i. writhe
j. pneumonia
k. poignant
l. arctic
m. arrangement
n. eighth
o. exhilarate
p. whether
q. rhyme
r. isthmus
s. exhausted
t. government
u. lightning
v. mathematician
w inhibition
x. undoubtedly
y. maligned

3.25 teacher check

3.26 Examples:
a. section added to a book or magazine
b. a housing for book, magazines and other reference material
c. the figure of a star (*) used in writing as a reference mark
d. a story or tale
e. a helping word as in <u>had</u> gone
f. words that describe or effect the meaning of other words

g. words that limit meaning

h. Az.

i. "Help!"

j. a word division or unit

k. a slanted type used for emphasis

l. use of capital letters

m. a punctuation mark (-)

n. can't, Jane's

o. <u>Un</u>cola, <u>re</u>take

p. attrac<u>tion</u>, achieve<u>ment</u>

q. can't, don't

r. marks indicating an after thought or aside "( )."

s. a form of a word showing ownership. <u>Jane's</u> book

t. an exchange of thoughts or messages with meaning

u. a motion of the body which has certain meaning

v. a style of speaking, word choice

w. following proper form, serious in tone

x. a word which has similar sound but is different in meaning and spelling

y. a word which is opposite in meaning

3.27 teacher check

3.28 teacher check

SELF TEST 1

1.01	meaning	1.023	false
1.02	inflections or combining forms	1.024	true
1.03	comparative	1.025	true
1.04	combining form	1.026	true
1.05	grammatical	1.027	false
1.06	d	1.028	true
1.07	j	1.029	kitten
1.08	l	1.030	cream
1.09	e	1.031	nail
1.010	a	1.032	hand
1.011	c	1.033	slow
1.012	i		
1.013	b		
1.014	h		

1.034 A syllable or syllables added to a root (base) to change its meaning or use ("prefix or suffix" counts 2 points).

1.015 k
1.016 b
1.017 d

1.035 The use of other parts of a sentence or paragraph to determine the meaning of an unfamiliar word.

1.018 a
1.019 a
1.020 d

1.036 An ending used to show case, gender, tense, mood, voice, number, comparison, (not all need to be listed).

1.021 true
1.022 true

1.037 The smallest part of a word that has meaning of its own (the smallest unit of meaning).

1.038 The highest degree of comparison of an adjective or adverb, used to compare more than two things.

SELF TEST 2

2.01	true	2.03	false
2.02	true	2.04	false

2.05   true
2.06   a. Listen attentively.
       b. Take notes.
       c. Ask questions.
2.07   combining forms
2.08   a participle

2.09   repeat
2.010 a. parent
       b. offspring
2.011 4
       2
       1
       5
       3

2.012 5
       1
       4
       2
       3
2.013 4
       2
       5
       3
       1

2.014 a comparison of like or similar things

2.015 two roots used together to form one
       word
2.016 a base, not necessarily a whole word, to
       which affixes are added to form new
       words

2.017 d
2.018 c
2.019 a

2.020 Hint:
       If the steps are followed out of order, the
       desired result may not be achieved.
       Following steps in order also helps
       assure that no step will be left out.

SELF TEST 3

3.01   communicate without words
3.02   a meaningful movement made
       with hands or body

3.03   personal appearance, facial
       expression, gesture, posture
3.04   a language or means of
       communication using special hand
       movements to represent letters,
       words, or concepts: alphabet-sign
       language

3.05   a word or sound which expresses a
       strong or sudden feeling

3.016 pantomime
3.017 face
3.018 Examples:
       a. smile/frown
       b. wink/grimace
       c. stick out tongue/ rolling eyes
3.019 Examples:
       a. Yippee!
       b. Oh Boy!
       c. Wow!
3.020 Examples:
       a. waving
       b. beckoning
       c. shaking hands/head.

3.06	h	3.010	e	3.013	k
3.07	j	3.011	c	3.014	l or i
3.08	g	3.012	a	3.015	d
3.09	i				

SELF TEST 1

1.01 Indo-European
1.02 a. Italo-Celtic
    b. Balto-Slavic
    c. Proto-Germanic
    d. Hellenic
    e. Indo-Iranian
1.03 Language changes with time; the English language has changed a great deal in 600 years.
1.04 a. Indo-European
    b. Proto-Germanic
    c. West Germanic, or Low German, Old English, Middle English
1.05 f
1.06 e
1.07 h
1.08 b
1.09 i
1.010 c
1.011 HG - High German
1.012 OF - Old French
1.013 Sp. - Spanish

1.014 Gk. - Greek
1.015 F - French
1.016 MF - Middle French
1.017 OE - Old English
1.018 OHG - Old High German
1.019 Du. - Dutch
1.020 Heb. - Hebrew
1.021 d
1.022 a
1.023 b
1.024 d
1.025 a

1.026 A form of language variation which can develop as a result of isolation. Dialect can be found in the Appalachian areas of Kentucky and West Virginia.

1.027 A scientist who studies records of languages and words.

SELF TEST 2

2.01 The <u>house</u> at the <u>end</u> of the <u>street</u> is being sold.
2.02 Did Carol call <u>you</u> yesterday?
2.03 When will the <u>books</u> be due?
2.04 The <u>teacher</u> told us to work quietly.
2.05 The <u>teapot</u> is older than <u>Grand-mother</u>.

2.06 Are you going to <u>her</u> <u>party</u>?
2.07 <u>He</u> wants us to be home by <u>ten</u> <u>o'clock</u>.
2.08 Won't <u>they</u> be angry?
2.09 The cat crept <u>stealthily</u> around the <u>dark</u> corner.
2.010 Mark closed the <u>heavy</u> <u>velvet</u> curtain <u>quietly</u>.

2.011 <u>Ten</u> <u>black</u> limousines headed the <u>long</u> parade.

2.012 Tony has a <u>cute</u> <u>little</u> <u>spotted</u> puppy.

2.013 He sneezed <u>noisily</u>.

2.014-2.018 Examples:

2.014 Example:
Indo European, Germanic, Old English, Middle English, Modern English

2.015 Early words starting with <u>f</u> changed to <u>b</u> in Latin. Germanic punctuation accented root syllables and used stress accent. Greek used pitch accent.

2.016 A dialect is a form of language variation which can develop as a result of isolation. A form of language has developed in the Appalachian areas of Kentucky and West Virginia.

2.017 By studying the changes words in related languages such as English, Latin, and Greek have undergone, scientists can trace a word back to its original form.

2.018 High German is the official and literary language used in Germany and Austria. Low German is spoken by the inhabitants of the Low Countries.

2.019 A noun names a person, place, or thing.

2.020 A pronoun stands for a noun.

2.021 A verb expresses action or state of being.

2.022 An adjective modifies a noun.

2.023 An adverb modifies a verb, adjective, or another adverb.

2.024 abstract

2.025 Either order:
  a. -self
  b. -selves

2.026 to modify a noun

2.027 Examples; any two:
  a. this, these
  b. that, those

2.028 linguist

2.029 Aramaic

2.030 auxiliary verb

2.031 indefinite

SELF TEST 3

3.01 c. Sanskrit
3.02 b. Indo-European
3.03 b. dialect

3.04 c. Old English

3.05 a. Greek
3.06 d. nouns, modifiers, and verbs

3.07 b. languages

3.08 c. express action
3.09 b. demonstrative
3.010 a. verbs, adjectives, and other adverbs

3.011 Examples; any two:
mother, three, seven

3.012 Examples; any three:
Indo-European, Proto-Germanic, West Germanic, Old English, Middle English

3.013 Examples:
   a. lovely, attractive
   b. modern
   c. well-behaved, delicious
   d. slim, slender
   e. small, tiny

3.014 c

3.015 b

3.016 a

3.017 b

3.018 c

3.019 b

3.020 c

3.021 a

3.022 a

3.023 b

3.024 Hint: It differs in dialect, expressions, accents, and various words.

SELF TEST 1

1.01 When I awoke, the day was gone. Looking down from where I lay, I saw a dog sitting on his haunches. His tongue, I believe, was bloody and hanging out of his mouth. He looked as if he were hungry. He had several wolf-like qualities: a gray coat, sharp claws, and yellow fangs. Those eyes - so cold and glinting - made me feel, dear reader, like the end was near. As I reached for a stick, he moved to the other side of the hill. Panting and hungry, he looked at me, a lonely, defenseless human, and he snarled. Well, I said my prayers, however, he simply turned his lean, shaggy body and and limped off into the woods.

        Total Points: 37

1.02 d

1.03 f

1.04 e

1.05 j
1.06 b
1.07 i
1.08 c

1.09 a

1.010 h
1.011 g

1.012 tonsils out, I have had

1.013 other side of the lake; consequently, there is

1.014 to visit; it is

1.015 the campers, the ranger

1.016 these items: a compass, a knapsack, a pick, and

1.017 You are, if I'm not mistaken, a good

1.018 His book, a soggy a mass of paper, was

1.019 tell us, Frank, why you're

1.020 Well, we can hardly

1.021 the time - this can

1.022-1.024 Examples:
1.022 Periods, question marks and exclamation points are used to mark the end of a complete thought.

1.023 Commas and semicolons are used to link independent clauses. Colons link independent clauses with a list which is dependent.

1.024 The dash and comma are used to mark a pause in thought for emphasis and clarity.

SELF TEST 2

2.01 b

2.02 f, g, h

2.03 b, d
2.04 a, c, e

2.05 a
Oh, I didn't. . .

2.06 c
. . . grammatical errors; many others. . . .

2.07   f
          . . . wish for: a lovely. . . .

2.08   b
          . . . just arrived, but we. . . .

2.09   f
          . . . favorite foods: steak, . . .

2.010   a
          . . . powerfully, he . . .

2.011   a
          . . . are finished, come to. . . .

2.012   e
          Come here, Dottie, and look. . . .

2.013   d
          Then Garth—he's the tall one—
          caught the pass and scored. . . .

2.014   e
          Her dress, soft and pretty,
          looked expensive.

2.015   false

2.016   false

2.017   false

2.018   true

2.019   false

2.020   false

2.021   true

2.022   true

2.023   false

2.024   true

2.025   a personal, humorous type of nonfiction
          with the purpose of entertaining

2.026   a formally constructed, serious type of
          writing having a thesis statement, logical
          organization and containing factual
          information whose purpose is to inform

2.027   a sentence stating an opinion or belief as
          the purpose for developing a paper,
          using facts, examples, and so on

2.028   a specific type or form of literature—a
          classification of types of writing such as
          the essay and poetry

2.029   a.   easy, conversational style
          b.   purpose of entertainment
          c.   humor
          d.   personal tone

2.030   a.   structured logical organization
          b.   informative purpose
          c.   a thesis statement
          d.   serious tone

SELF TEST 1

1.01	S
1.02	A
1.03	S
1.04	S
1.05	H
1.06	A
1.07	H
1.08	A
1.09	H
1.010	A
1.011	synonyms
1.012	homonyms
1.013	syn
1.014	antonyms
1.015	dictionary
1.016	Thesaurus
1.017	homonyms
1.018	directions
1.019	homonyms
1.020	antonym

1.021	syn
1.022	hom
1.023	hom
1.024	syn
1.025	ant
1.026	ceiling
1.027	rein or reign
1.028	meddle
1.029	night
1.030	dye
1.031	pray
1.032	altar
1.033	some
1.034	course
1.035	bow
1.036	fare
1.037	board, meet
1.038	sum, one
1.039	heard, course
1.040	by, altar, To

SELF TEST 2

2.01	c. plān
2.02	e. cat
2.03	a. a mung′ (a məng′)
2.04	b. bor′ der
2.05	d. fare
2.06	sub ject′
2.07	ob′ ject
2.08	in sert′
2.09	re cord′
2.010	ex per′ i ment
2.011	sur′ prise
2.012	ro tate′
2.013	a. diacritical
	b. respelling
2.014	macron
2.015	breve

2.016	accent
2.017	homonyms
2.018	thesaurus
2.019	opposite
2.020	antonym
2.021	true
2.022	false
2.023	true
2.024	true
2.025	false
2.026	true
2.027	true
2.028	false
2.029	true
2.030	false

SELF TEST 3

3.01	standard	3.020	c	
3.02	antonyms	3.021	false	
3.03	homonyms	3.022	true	
3.04	Thesaurus	3.023	true	
3.05	macron	3.024	false	
3.06	homonyms	3.025	true	
3.07	meanings	3.026	true	
3.08	diacritical marks and accent marks	3.027	true	
3.09	long	3.028	true	
3.010	sets	3.029	true	
3.011	sit	3.030	true	
3.012	May	3.031	false	
3.013	taught	3.032	false	
3.014	fare	3.033	false	
3.015	b	3.034	true	
3.016	e or d	3.035	false	
3.017	d or e	3.036	false	
3.018	f	3.037	true	
3.019	a	3.038	false	

SELF TEST 1

1.01 d

1.02 a

1.03 c

1.04 b

1.05 b

1.06 a

1.07 c

1.08 f

1.09 e

1.010 f, e

1.011 d, e

1.012 a'

1.013 e

1.014 b

1.015 My forty-year-old aunt has been in twenty-five countries.

1.016 Jerry's beat-up-looking Ford has a custom-built engine.

1.017 Her daughter-in-law's house had a make-yourself-at-home look.

1.018 His holier-than-thou attitude seemed rather unChristian.

1.019 The store's mid-July sale netted the owners ten-thousand dollars.

1.020 The computer's tapes became tangled in the programmer's fingers.

1.021 a. child's
      b. children
      c. children's

1.022 a. man's
      b. men
      c. men's

1.023 a. wolf's
      b. wolves
      c. wolves'

1.024 a. king's
      b. kings
      c. kings'

1.025 a. Thomas' (Thomas's)
      b. Thomases
      c. Thomases'

1.026 a. cousin's
      b. cousins
      c. cousins'

1.027 a. monkey's
      b. monkeys
      c. monkeys'

1.028 a. secretary's
      b. secretaries
      c. secretaries'

1.029 a. fish's
      b. fish or fishes
      c. fish's

1.030 a. tomato's
      b. tomatoes
      c. tomatoes'

1.031 My sister (the tall one) took Uncle George and Aunt Ruth to see Life with Father that was performed by the Roadside Theater.

1.032 The Last of the Mohicans by James F. Cooper has been translated into French, German, and Swedish.

1.033 Tom's Easter vacation wasn't spent in California.

1.034 Jill screamed, "It's alive and breathing!"

1.035 I'll; can't

1.036 wasn't; He's

1.037 Doesn't

1.038 They're

SELF TEST 2

2.01 e

2.02 a

2.03 i

2.04 g

2.05 c

2.06 h

2.07 b

2.08 d
2.09 f
2.010 j
2.011 a. possession
     b. contractions
     c. dialectal
2.012 a. compound words
     b. syllables
     Either order:
     c. numbers or figures
     d. prefixes and suffixes to
        root words

2.013 Any order:
     a. direct quotations
     b. chapters
     c. paintings
     d. songs or articles, short stories

2.014 Either order:
     a. incidental remarks
     b. numbers or letters

2.015 Any order:
     a. books, long plays, newspapers, magazines
     b. ships, trains, planes, motion pictures
     c. foreign words or phrases
     d. words used as words or letters used as letters

2.016 Any order:
     a. first word of a sentence
     b. names of companies or organizations
     c. names of countries, cities, continents, etc.
     d. important words in titles
     e. names of historical events, documents, and periods of history
     f. days of week, months, holidays

2.017 "Charlie," Jill called. "Come here!"

2.018 I read "I Fool Pap and Get Away" in The Adventures of Huckleberry Finn.

2.019 The women's voices reached their mothers-in-law.
2.020 a. don't
     b. won't
     c. can't

2.021 a. brother-in-law's
     b. wives'
     c. sheep's

SELF TEST 3

3.01 accept
3.02 complemented
3.03 council
3.04 eligible

3.05 concave
3.06 All together
3.07 indignant
3.08 weather

3.09   principal

3.010 explicit

3.011 homonyms

3.012 antonyms

3.013 synonyms

3.014 vicarious

3.015 direct quotation

3.016 speech

3.017 being familiar with the subject

3.018 an apostrophe

3.019 a. an apostrophe
       b. an apostrophe + s

3.020 a. know the subject,
       b. show enthusiasm,
       c. use meaningful gestures,
       d. use pleasant, expressive voice, and
       e. set a pleasing pace, (or speak clearly, use humor carefully)

3.021 Aunt Annie was rather down-in-the mouth until her mother-in-law gave her and Uncle Bob a ticket to Hawaii for Christmas. At the bon voyage party aboard the Hawaiian Queen, Aunt Annie told her, "We're finally goin', thanks to you."

SELF TEST 1

1.01	true	1.023	where
1.02	false	1.024	ship
1.03	false	1.025	there
1.04	true	1.026	knight
1.05	true	1.027	it
1.06	true	1.028	heaven
1.07	false	1.029	truth
1.08	true	1.030	forgive
1.09	false	1.031	fourteenth
1.010	false	1.032	London
1.011	b	1.033	French
1.012	d	1.034	comitatus
1.013	f	1.035	Bede
1.014	a	1.036	wise-sayings
1.015	k	1.037	me
1.016	i	1.038	vowels
1.017	c	1.039	culture
1.018	e	1.040	French or Latin or both
1.019	j	1.041	The place where an Anglo-Saxon ship burial was found in 1939.
1.020	g		
1.021	day	1.042	Because it uncovered many Anglo-Saxon artifacts that are similar to those described in Anglo-Saxon poems.
1.022	man		

SELF TEST 2

2.01	g	2.05	e
2.02	c	2.06	a
2.03	k	2.07	j
2.04	h	2.08	b

2.09   l

2.010   d

2.011   Any order:
- a. coordinating conjunctions
- b. correlative conjunctions
- c. conjunctive adverbs

2.012   less

2.013   Any order:
- a. adverb clauses
- b. adjective clauses
- c. phrases
- d. appositives

2.014   perform a similar function

2.015   correlative conjunctions

2.016   d

2.017   b

2.018   c

2.019   d

2.020   a

2.021   a

2.022   a

2.023   Examples; Any order:
- a. and
- b. but
- c. so
- d. yet
- or for
-     nor
-     or

2.024   Any order:
- a. both. . .and
- b. either. . .or
- c. neither. . .nor
- d. not only. . .but also
- or whether. . .or

2.025   Examples; Any order:
- a. also
- b. furthermore
- c. anyway
- d. hence
- e. however
- f. still
- or then, nevertheless, thus,
- or any others listed on page 23.

2.026   An elegy is a poem about a serious subject.

2.027   The *comitatus* was the relationship between a leader and his men. The leader provided for and protected his men in return for their loyalty and military support.

SELF TEST 3

3.01	c	3.013	d	3.025	true
3.02	e	3.014	a	3.026	setting (location)
3.03	h	3.015	d	3.027	time
3.04	f	3.016	b	3.028	personal life
3.05	j	3.017	a	3.029	turning point
3.06	a	3.018	c	3.030	theme
3.07	i	3.019	b		
3.08	g	3.020	d		
3.09	d	3.021	true		
3.010	b	3.022	false		
3.011	a	3.023	false		
3.012	c	3.024	false		

SELF TEST 1

1.01   false

1.02   true

1.03   false

1.04   false

1.05   true

1.06   because they may be misleading or absurd

1.07   defining a word by its context

1.08   One might think of alcohol; in reality it might mean all types of juices or water after hard work.

1.09   wording that attempts to influence someone's actions because of the future

1.010 It prepares us for the future. It may make false promises and disillusion us.

1.011 f

1.012 b

1.013 a

1.014 b

1.015 d

1.016 b

1.017 a

1.018 a

1.019 c

1.020 e

1.021 d

1.022 b

1.023 a. This first one is an emotional appeal. Since we like to feel good about what we eat, perhaps we will buy this product.

       b. Since everyone wants to be doing the popular thing, buying this bed will help the buyer to feel he belongs.

       c. The public desires to identify with famous personalities. Women especially would buy this.

       d. This example of the black or white fallacy leaves no choice. Either you get the job done or you do not.

       e. This example of name calling encourages a buyer to purchase this product over another well-known brand.

1.024 b

1.025 a

1.026 d

1.027 c

1.028 d

SELF TEST 2

2.01   g

2.02   a

2.03   b

2.04   f

2.05   j

2.06   i

2.07   c

2.08   h

2.09   d

2.010 e

2.011 Men tend to be at greater risk of heart attack than women.

2.012 To decrease the risk of heart attack, man should learn all he can about good habits in matters of health.

2.013 expository

2.014 a. narrative
       b. descriptive

2.015 a. unity
       b. coherence

2.016 chronological

2.017 spatial

2.018 general to particular

2.019 particular to general

2.020 comparison/contrast

2.021-2.023 Any order:

2.021 continuity of thought

2.022 pronoun reference

2.023 transition words

2.024 First, Since, Secondly, Equally important, In fact, therefore, Finally

2.025 to 2.029 Examples:

2.025 The question is irrelevant to what we are studying.

2.026 Ruth's recipe for fudge is infallible.

2.027 Paragraph three is filled with ambiguity.

2.028 John's theme is a good example of continuity of ideas.

2.029 The subtle suggestion was hardly noticeable.

SELF TEST 3

3.01   c

3.02   b

3.03   a

3.04   e

3.05   f

3.06   d

3.07   h

3.08   i

3.09   g

3.010 j

3.011 false

3.012 false

3.013 false

3.014 true

3.015 false

3.016 true

3.017 true

3.018 false

3.019 false

3.020 false

3.021 true

3.022 false

3.023 true

3.024   introduction, body, conclusion

3.025   The thesis of a theme states what
the writer intends to prove.

3.026   Open with general statements working
to the thesis.

3.027   It introduces the subject and gets
to the point of the theme.

3.028   With reason you can tell why something is so. With examples you
can prove your point with actual
fact. Incidents also give proof
with actual circumstances.

3.029   They are used for coherence because
they tie one paragraph to another.

3.030   It restates the thesis and closes
the paper by summarizing what has
been said.

3.031   Don't just dully repeat the thesis;
don't give a repetition of facts
word for word; have an imaginative
conclusion.

3.032 b. – 3.041 b. Examples:

3.032   a. FRAG
b. Although he rarely ever goes,
my father enjoys baseball games.

3.033   a. FRAG
b. I was almost asleep, when the
stone hit the window.

3.034   a. FRAG
b. George is happiest when he is
fishing in the mountain stream
and camping in rough terrain.

3.035   a. RO
b. . . . aspect of life. I believe . . .

3.036   a. RO
b. . . . I've ever seen, and I
think . . .

3.037   a. RO
b. . . . to discover. If someone . . .

3.038   a. RO
b. . . . are overreacting? A lot of . . .

3.039   a. FRAG
b. . . . on the stage, deserted by . . .

3.040   a. FRAG
b. . . . those seasons. Regardless of. . .
or seasons, when regardless. . .

3.041   a. FRAG
b. I want to tell you. . .

3.042 – 3.046 Examples:

3.042   The inference was that we should always
be punctual.

3.043   An element of ambiguity was present
in his speech.

3.044   My being there is irrelevant to your
going.

3.045   The literal meaning of this statement
has been omitted.

3.046   Mary writes in clear and concise
sentences.

SELF TEST 1

1.01	true	
1.02	false	
1.03	false	
1.04	true	
1.05	true	
1.06	false	
1.07	true	
1.08	true	
1.09	false	
1.010	false	
1.011	b	
1.012	c	
1.013	f	
1.014	a	
1.015	e	
1.016	f	
1.017	d	
1.018	full block	
1.019	$8\frac{1}{2}''$ X 11"	
1.020	one or two inches	
1.021	one-half	
1.022	business	
1.023	personal	

1.024-1.029 Examples:

1.024 When an error has been made, an adjustment letter attempts to correct the problem.

1.025 An order letter is a way of ordering or purchasing merchandise.

1.026 Letters of application are used to apply for a job, for a place in a school or college, or for something competitive.

1.027 A friendly letter is a way of telling what has happened to you. It is written to a relative or friend you have not seen for some time.

1.028 This kind of letter is used to invite someone overnight for a special occasion.

1.029 This letter is used to thank someone for a gift, a special favor, or a treat.

1.030 Example:
The ability to write good letters, whether for business or for social reasons, is an asset. When one needs to do so, he should be able to write an effective letter using correct form and structure to convey his message clearly, neatly, and respectfully. A properly written letter will leave a favorable impression with the receiver, and its message will be taken seriously.

SELF TEST 2

2.01	true	2.08	false
2.02	false	2.09	true
2.03	false	2.010	true
2.04	true	2.011	b
2.05	true	2.012	d
2.06	true	2.013	a
2.07	false	2.014	e

2.015 c

2.016 b

2.017 e

2.018 a

2.019 c

2.020 d

2.021-2.024   Any order:

2.021 heading

2.022 inside address

2.023 body

2.024 closing

2.025 inside address

2.026-2.030   Examples:

2.026 nervousness

2.027 interest

2.028 rejection, denial, disagreement

2.029 anger

2.030 uncertainty or shyness

2.031-2.035   Examples:

2.031 unsure or nervous

2.032 emphatic or excited

2.033 angry or upset

2.034 tenderness

2.035 sarcasm or irony

SELF TEST 3

3.01 true

3.02 false

3.03 false

3.04 true

3.05 false

3.06 false

3.07 false

3.08 true

3.09 true

3.010 false

3.011 d

3.012 h

3.013 b

3.014 i

3.015 a

3.016 k

3.017 c

3.018 f

3.019 e

3.020 j

3.021 salutation

3.022 heading

3.023 closing

3.024 body

3.025 inside address

3.026 recognition

3.027 literal

3.028 inferred
       or implied
       or code words

3.029 nonverbal

3.030 figures of speech

3.031 Business letters consist of adjustment, order, and application letters.

3.032 Personal letters may be friendly letters, letters of invitation, or thank-you letters.

3.033 He understands the physical process of listening, the interpretation of literal and implied meanings, and the meanings of figures of speech. He is also aware of voice tone, gesture, and other nonverbal means of communicating. The most important characteristic is the desire to listen attentively.

3.034 They both have a heading, a salutation, a body, a closing, and a signature.

3.035 Any order:
a. Time
b. Newsweek
c. U.S. News and World Report

3.036 Any order:
a. primary
b. secondary
c. reference
d. general

3.037 Any order:
a. who
b. what
c. when
d. where
e. why
f. how

SELF TEST 1

1.01 the study of languages

1.02 outdated

1.03 collected, articulated

1.04 complete, not shortened

1.05 to send or receive from a source

1.06 false

1.07 false

1.08 true

1.09 false

1.010 true

1.011 true

1.012 true

1.013 false

1.014 false

1.015 false

1.016 f

1.017 h

1.018 c

1.019 d

1.020 n

1.021 k

1.022 b

1.023 j

1.024 a

1.025 l

1.026 g

1.027 It allowed more people access to more books that offered examples of proper grammar and sentence structure.

1.028 It is designed for informal communication, usually verbal. Sometimes it is used to confuse a third party who is unaware of the words. It is often reflective of a particular group of people, such as laborers, musicians, and so on.

1.029 A living language is a contemporary language, still in popular use. It is still changing naturally according to the needs of its people. A dead language does not change because it is not written or spoken today except by scholars.

SELF TEST 2

2.01 is

2.02 his

2.03 are

2.04 anything

2.05 is

2.06 forgot

2.07 is

2.08 have

2.09 is

2.010 his

2.011 A piece of toast stuck in his throat while he was gulping down his breakfast.

2.012 After many hours of prayer, Tom felt the problem resolved in his mind.

2.013 When cleaning, I get dust in my eyes.

2.014 Unrolling his sleeping bag, Tim thought the night was strangely quiet.

2.015 One should read his assignment in the textbook.

2.016 b

2.017 b

2.018 a

2.019 b

2.020 a

2.021 b

2.022 b

2.023 a

2.024 b

2.025 b

2.026 are

2.027 any

2.028 have

2.029 his

2.030 he

2.031 were

2.032 is

2.033 his

2.034 were

2.035 were

2.036 linguistics

2.037 a. Normans
      b. French

2.038 etymology

2.039 slang

2.040 a. printing press
      b. Gutenburg

2.041 Either order:
      a. John Wycliffe
      b. King James

2.042 a. living
      b. dead

SELF TEST 3

3.01 false

3.02 false

3.03 true

3.04 false

3.05 true

3.06 false

3.07 true

3.08 false

3.09 false

3.010 c

3.011 k

3.012 h

3.013 f

3.014 g

3.015 d

3.016 e

3.017 j

3.018 b

3.019   i

3.020   a statement of direction or
purpose to be presented at the
beginning of the speech

3.021   the study of the origin or
derivation of words

3.022   the rules for writing or speaking
properly

3.023   the careful formation of words

3.024   Any order:
   a. thesis
   b. main body
   c. conclusion

3.025   Any order:
   a. exposition
   b. process and analysis
   c. definition
   d. persuasion
   e. expression

3.026   Any order:
   a. dangling participles
   b. dangling infinitives
   c. dangling elliptical phrases

3.027   double negative

3.028   an antecedent

3.029   Any order:
   a. indicative
   b. subjunctive
   c. imperative

3.030   archaic

3.031   Either order:
   a. slang
   b. jargon

3.032   living

3.033   obsolete

3.034   linguistics

3.035   Neither of us is going to the store.

3.036   When one is an athlete, he
should never stay out late at
night.

3.037   Forgetting he was going to meet
his boss, he sent everything
to the cleaners except his
jogging suit.

3.038   Sit still and behave in
front of company.

SELF TEST 1

1.01 true

1.02 true

1.03 false

1.04 false

1.05 true

1.06 false

1.07 true

1.08 false

1.09 false

1.010 false

1.011 b

1.012 g

1.013 d

1.014 a

1.015 c

1.016 k

1.017 f

1.018 j

1.019 h

1.020 i

1.021 verb

1.022 adjective

1.023 noun

1.024 pronoun

1.025 adverb

1.026 pronoun

1.027 pronoun

1.028 noun

1.029 A noun is a part of speech that names persons, places, and things.

1.030 A verb is a part of speech that shows action or a state of being.

1.031 A pronoun is a part of speech that takes the place of a noun.

1.032 An adjective is a part of speech that describes nouns and tells which one, what kind, and how many.

1.033 An adverb is a part of speech that modifies verbs, adjectives, and other adverbs, answering when?, where?, how?, and how much?.

1.034 The letters of an abbreviation used as a word make an acronym.

1.035 Etymology is the study of word histories.

1.036 Noah Webster introduced the first United States dictionary.

1.037 subject, predicate

SELF TEST 2

2.01 true

2.02 true

2.03 true

2.04 true

2.05 true

2.06 true

2.07 true

2.08 false

2.09 true

2.010 false

2.011 f

2.012 c

2.013 e

2.014 h

2.015 a

2.016 g

2.017 d

2.018 k

2.019 j

2.020 i

2.021 Any order:
  a. facial expressions
  b. gestures
  c. body movements

2.022 Any order:
  a. inform
  b. persuade
  c. entertain

2.023 toward the last person in the back of the audience

2.024 Example; either order:
  a. to make himself understood
  b. to speak as an oracle in praise of God

2.025 Either order:
  a. verbal
  b. nonverbal

2.026 Either order:
  a. dictionary
  b. thesaurus

2.027 a. I. Introduction, or thesis paragraph
  b. II. Paragraphs of detail supporting thesis
  c. III. Conclusion, or clincher paragraph

2.028 Any order:
  a. topic sentence
  b. all sentences relate to topic
  c. paragraph has a specific purpose
  d. coherence

2.029 Example:
Both the paragraph and the theme are serious forms of writing about one topic written for a specific purpose. Each must have a main idea or thesis and supporting detail for that thesis. Each has a conclusion, or clincher, which restates the thesis.

2.030 Example:
Linking expressions connect the ideas and provide smooth transitions between sentences and paragraphs.

2.031 One; I; picnic.; Mother; cake. ; My; sister-in-law; cola.; Dad; way.; Rodney,; brother,; I; Mom; food.; Just; I; Linda's; salad,; raining.; "Quick!"; Mother; shouted.; "Get; inside!"; We; camper.; Doesn't; picnic?

SELF TEST 3

3.01   l

3.02   c

3.03   e

3.04   g

3.05   h

3.06   b

3.07   i

3.08   f/a

3.09   d

3.010 a/f

3.011 k

3.012 Indo-European

3.013 a. dictionary
       b. thesaurus

3.014 synonym

3.015 subject

3.016 verbal

3.017 read

3.018 Any order:
       a. who
       b. what
       c. when
       d. where
       e. why
       f. how

3.019 first

3.020 inverted pyramid

3.021 A fact can be proved; an opinion is a belief.

3.022 Example:
       The main purpose of a serious
       essay is to inform using a logical
       presentation of factual information.

3.023 Any order:
       a. setting
       b. time
       c. personal life
       d. turning points
       e. theme

3.024 Any order:
       a. topic sentence
       b. all sentences relate to topic
       c. paragraph has a specific purpose
       d. coherence

3.025 Either order:
       a. chronological order
       b. spatial order

3.026 Any order:
       a. run-on
       b. fragment
       c. comma splice

3.027 Any order:
       a. business-adjustment,
          application, order
       b. personal-friendly, thank-you,
          invitation

3.028 The pentad is a five-part method
       of organizing a speech.

3.029 Sequence is the order in which
       events or items are arranged.

3.030 A thesis is a statement
       of purposes or direction
       used in a speech or a
       composition.

1. false

2. false

3. false
4. true
5. false

6. a

7. c
8. b

9. c

10. g

11. a
12. e

13. f

14. d
15. c
16. c
17. b
18. d
19. c
20. a
21. c

22. Examples: Referees and umpires signal decisions. Players signal time-outs. Pitchers and catchers signal each other.
23. Examples: codes and signals- Morse Code, flag signals, lights, flares
24. You will be able to determine a person's meaning or message by his appearance, his posture, gestures, and facial expression as well as his words.
25. Examples; any order:
    a. through smiling and facial expressions
    b. by interjection (yeh!), a whistle or laugh
    c. by posture - jumping up and down, clapping hands
26. Examples; any order:
    a. raise your hand, wave arms
    b. stand up - tap someone on shoulders
    c. whistle, scream, shout
27. critical
28. an analogy
29. inflection
30. participle
31. context clue

1.   m

2.   g

3.   j

4.   i

5.   b

6.   a

7.   d

8.   f

9.   h

10. c

11. l

12. k

13. Indo-European

Examples (14 - 18):
14. a. brilliant
     b. multi-colored

15. a. dismal
     b. remote

16. a. dilapidated
     b. picturesque

17. a. colorful
     b. whirling

18. a. shaggy
     b. enormous

19. noun

20. pronoun

21. adjective

22. adverb

23. adjective

24. verb

25. verb

26. pronoun

27. noun

28. adjective

29. Example:
     a spoken or written form of communi-
     cation using agreed-upon symbols for
     ideas or concepts

30. a. Proto-Germanic
     b. West Germanic
     c. Low German
     d. Old English
     e. Middle English

31. Language is important to man-
     kind because it allows him a
     way to communicate his thoughts,
     feelings, and knowledge to
     others.

32. Examples:
     some dictionaries; book of etymology

1. The Russian defector, a sailor who had jumped ship near Canada, became a Christian.

   comma used with an appositive

2. Huckleberry Finn is a favorite book of many people; it also has a very serious message.

   semicolon used as a link between two independent clauses

3. Some people try to slalom when the water is calm, yet that's when many accidents occur.

   comma used with a conjunction to link two independent clauses

4. The blazing sun, gnats, and stretches of sand - everything added to the fugitive's misery.

   dash used for a summarizing phrase

5. Intending to catch his brother by surprise, Ted hid near the model airplane.

   comma used with introductory participial phrase

6. As if sky diving wasn't enough, Chuck now wanted to try free fall!

   comma used with introductory subordinate clause

7. I fell—wouldn't you know—into the deepest part of the river.

   dash used for sudden break in thought

8. The plan was this: divide the troops, surround the enemy, and capture the headquarters.

   colon used before a list of items

9. The tiny, insignificant twitch of his right eyebrow gave him away to the detective, a man about forty.

   comma used with appositive

10. The camera fell into the pool; however, it worked better after it got soaked!

    semicolon used for certain conjunctives and used to introduce a qualifying statement

11. d
12. c
13. a
14. a
15. d

16. The essay deals with a limited topic and informs or entertains the reader. It is usually brief and can be read in one sitting. It is found in many magazines today.
17. structured organization
18. follows a thesis
19. mainly informative
20. serious tone
21. often humorous
22. much more personal
23. a free, unstructured style
24. entertains rather than informs

25. I
26. F
27. F
28. I
29. I
30. F
31. F
32. I
33. F
34. I

1.	d	21.	true
2.	f	22.	false
3.	i	23.	false
4.	b	24.	true
5.	g	25.	true
6.	h	26.	standard
7.	j	27.	synonyms
8.	a	28.	homonyms
9.	e	29.	communicate
10.	c	30.	antonyms
11.	A	31.	course
12.	A	32.	contraction
13.	H	33.	arid
14.	H	34.	Either order:
15.	A		a. by the diacritical markings
16.	H		b. by the respelling (phonetic spelling) of the word
17.	S	35.	Either order:
18.	S		a. dictionary
19.	H		b. thesaurus (Roget's International Thesaurus)
20.	S		

1. H
2. A
3. S
4. A
5. H
6. A
7. H
8. S

9. A

10. H

11. c

12. e

13. a

14. b
15. b

16. c
17. d
18. a
19. b
20. d
21. deductive
22. dairy
23. indigent

24. italicized
25. underlining
26. apostrophe's
27. capitalizing
28. hyphens
29. set off by quotation marks
30. underlining or italics (either one)
31. Any order:
   a. know subject,
   b. show enthusiasm,
   c. use meaningful gestures,
   d. use pleasant, expressive voice,
   e. set a pleasing pace,
   f. speak clearly, and
   g. use humor carefully

32. Example:
   speak wisely, not foolishly, speak to build up, not tear down, speak purely.

33. Example:
   A person has an experience vicariously when he reads or hears something another person has experienced.

34. Example:
   Punctuation makes written and spoken language clear or understandable.

35. pound
36. cash on delivery
37. medical doctor
38. boulevard

1.	b		21.	true
2.	a		22.	true
3.	c		23.	false
4.	c		24.	false
5.	a		25.	true
6.	c		26.	false
7.	d		27.	true
8.	b		28.	false
9.	d		29.	true
10.	c		30.	false

11. 1066

12. Celts or Britons

13. Sutton Hoo

14. Beowulf

15. an elegy

16. Alfred

17. dialect

18. French

19. Either order:
   a. his
   b. him
   or me, he, we, us

20. where

31.-33. Examples:

31. a story, or connected narrative that a person writes about his own life; it reveals the author's personal feelings and thoughts

32. an event or situation in a story or autobiography which changes the lives of one or more people

33. a truth the author expresses about life as he sees it; it may influence the reader's ideas

34. Some Old English forms have been retained. Literature and early tradition is preserved for later times.

35. gain insight into famous people, times; a source of inspiration; excitement and entertainment

1. true
2. true

3. false
4. false

5. true
6. false
7. false

8. true

9. false

10. true

11. b

12. b

13. d

14. b

15. b

16. a

17. a

18. a

19. d

20. f

21. a. introduction
    b. body
    c. conclusion

22. the subject of your paper; what you're trying to prove

23. go from general to particular (inverted triangle)

24. you make your case stronger as you disprove opposing views

25. a. reasons
    b. examples
    c. incidents

26. from particular to general - (triangle)

27. While walking through the old English castle, I saw a door that looked as though no one ever used it. Naturally, I opened it. Then, suddenly, the door slammed behind me and left me in the dark, a little anxious, and not to mention terrified, tourist. I banged on the door and screamed unashamedly for help. Then I sheepishly grinned as the tour guide yanked open the door. While I waded through stares of hundreds of curious tourists, I decided castles were dumb places to visit.

28. g

29. c

30. a

31. f

32. h

33. d

34. j

35. b

36. k

37. i

1. true

2. true

3. false

4. false
5. false

6. true

7. true
8. false

9. true
10. false

11. d

12. j
13. a

14. k
15. g

16. h

17. c

18. f

19. b

20. i
21. simile

22. metaphor

23. gestures
24. inference
25. implying
26. propaganda

27. Any order:
   a. heading
   b. inside address
   c. salutation
   d. body
   e. closing
   f. signature

28. Any order:
   a. adjustment
   b. order
   c. application

29. Any order:
   a. friendly
   b. invitation
   c. thank-you

30. Any order:
   a. literal
   b. implied
   c. figurative

31. Either order:
   a. tone of voice
   b. movement of body

32. Any order:
   a. understand process of listening
   b. understand literal and implied meanings
   c. understand use of figures of speech
   d. can interpret such nonverbal messages as gestures and expressions
   e. can interpret voice tone
   f. wants to listen attentively

33. a. Mrs. Sally R. Hansen
   b. Credit Department Manager
   c. Fleming's Department Store
   d. 1234 Fourth Avenue
   e. Hometown, Iowa 54321

1. j

2. d

3. b

4. c

5. f

6. e

7. i

8. g

9. h

10. a

11. true

12. true

13. true

14. false
15. false
16. true
17. false
18. true
19. true
20. false
21. Any order:
    a. thesis
    b. main body
    c. conclusion
22. Any order:
    a. what?
    b. who or what acted?
    c. what setting?
    d. by what means?
    e. for what purpose?

23. Any order:
    a. exposition
    b. process and analysis
    c. definition
    d. persuasion
    e. expression

24. Any order:
    a. double negatives
    b. dangling modifiers
    c. faulty (shift) in person and number
    d. faulty (shift) in subject and verb agreement

25. b

26. a

27. b

28. b

29. b

30. a
31. a
32. a

1. c
2. d
3. g
4. e
5. j
6. h
7. b
8. a
9. i
10. f
11. true
12. false
13. false
14. true
15. false
16. true
17. true
18. true
19. false
20. true
21. Example:
   a fact can be proven, but an opinion is a belief.
22. alphabetical listing of words, pronunciation, definitions, correct spelling, part of speech, etymology
23. Noah Webster
24. Any order:
   a. topic sentence
   b. all sentences relate to topic (unity)
   c. written for a specific purpose
   d. coherence
25. O
26. F
27. O
28. F
29. Her; sister-in-law; editor-in-chief; paper.
30. "Help me!"; cried.; "I'm falling!"
31. Can; George,; Mary,; Fred; coming?
32. a. dictionary
   b. 1806
33. Roget's International Thesaurus
34. Any order:
   a. to inform
   b. to persuade
   c. to entertain
35. Either order:
   a. verbal
   b. nonverbal
36. An autobiography is a nonfiction narrative written by the author about his own personal life.
37. Nonverbal communication communicates ideas by use of gestures, facial gestures, facial expressions, body language, or pantomime.

1.   true
2.   false
3.   true
4.   true
5.   true
6.   b. milk
7.   c. hand
8.   c. winter
9.   d. knife
10. d
11. g
12. a
13. b
14. f
15. c
16. d. morpheme
17. c. prefix or suffix
18. c. analogies
19. b. attentiveness
20. a. order
21. d. necessary

22. Example:
     A system of hand signals was devised. It is made up of special positions of hands and fingers that stand for concepts, words, or letters of the alphabet.

23. Example:
     Interjections are sounds which are exclaimed. They are frequently accompanied by words (wow, boo, ha).

24. Example:
     Root words are the building blocks for the formation of other words.

25. Examples; any order:
     a. happiness
     b. sadness
     c. fear

26. Examples; any order
     a. referees and umpires
     b. military
     c. policemen

27. Example:
     Be sure the listener is attentive. Give the directions clearly in proper order of sequence. Answer any questions the listener asks.

1. j
2. m
3. l
4. k
5. a
6. c
7. e
8. i
9. d
10. g
11. b
12. h
13. Semitic
14. Examples:
    a. rugged
    b. treacherous
15. Examples:
    a. surprise
    b. exciting
16. Examples:
    a. energetic
    b. excited
17. Examples:
    a. gorgeous
    b. spacious
18. Examples:
    a. thrilling
    b. inspiring
19. noun
20. pronoun
21. adjective
22. adverb
23. adjective
24. verb
25. verb
26. verb
27. noun
28. adverb
29. Example:
    Language is one of man's most distinguishing features. It is how man gives and receives messages.
30. Example:
    Man has an analytical brain. This brain can sort and separate and develop a language system.
31. Example:
    Languages change at different rates in different areas. These changes account for the many dialects we have in America.
32. Example:
    The Germanic groups subdivided. The West Germanic language was further subdivided into dialects including High German and Low German.

1. Have you ever read *Moby Dick* , a book about a white whale?
   comma needed to set off appositive

2. I climbed seven flights of stairs in ten minutes; Mother took the elevator and had to wait for me at the top.
   semicolon used between two closely related independent clauses

3. I would like to go to the park with you, but my bicycle is broken.
   comma used with a conjunction to link two independent clauses

4. The ants, flies, and the light rain— everything seemed to go wrong on our camping trip last weekend.
   commas within a series and dash used for a summarizing phrase

5. Waiting for the girl to take his order, Jimmy hungrily studied the menu.
   comma used with introductory participial phrase

6. The room–what a mess–had been searched by the intruder.
   dashes used to show a sudden break in thought

7. Although he had only been there five minutes, Dave left their house.
   comma used with introductory subordinate clause

8. Mr. Brown offered a reward to the boy or girl bringing in the most aluminum cans; therefore, Frank and I have been picking up cans in the park all morning.
   semicolon used before certain conjunctives used to introduce a qualifying statement and comma used after conjunction

9. A good pizza should contain the following ingredients: cheese, tomato sauce, Italian sausage, olives, and spices.
   colon used before a list of items

10. Walter Jamison, an outstanding businessman and a devout Christian, has been elected president of the local businessmen's club.
    comma used to set off appositive

11. Either order:
    a. declarative
    b. imperative

12. interrogative

13. a significant pause or interruption in thought

14. before a list

15. participle

16. d

17. c

18. f

19. e

20. b

21. Any order:
    a. may have a serious tone
    b. follows a thesis
    c. has a structured organization
    d. is mainly informative

22. Any order:
    a. has a humorous tone
    b. is personal
    c. has a free, unstructured style
    d. entertains

23. Any order:
    a. reasons
    b. examples
    c. incidents

24. Example:
    The purpose is generally stated in the thesis statement which usually appears in the introductory paragraph.

1. synonyms
2. macron
3. antonyms
4. antonyms
5. Example:
   respect
6. Standard English
7. true
8. true
9. false
10. false
11. true
12. c
13. f
14. e
15. a
16. d
17. b
18. should
19. effect
20. invitation
21. sit
22. taught
23. He finished his geography *course* in one semester.
24. Example:
   Lynn *enjoys* asparagus in salads.
25. Example:
   Jerry will be *here* in an hour.

26. Example:
   We had an *exciting* time at the fair.
27. true
28. true
29. false
30. Example:
   Read the entire application, test, or set of directions before writing anything. Answer each question or complete each step to the best of your ability. Be specific. Do not leave any blanks or omit any steps. Work neatly. Check over your work. Correct any mistakes.

1. Examples:
    a. error
    b. inquire
    c. cavity
2. Examples:
    a. ascend
    b. sickly
    c. spicy
3. a. there
    b. hair
    c. mane
4. Examples:
    a. it should give good reports
    b. it should be gracious
    c. it should answer rightly
5. Any order, any three:
    a. familiarity with the subject
    b. humor
    c. enthusiasm
    or use of appropriate gestures, pleasing voice patterns, good enunciation
6. Either order:
    a. show possession
    b. form contractions
7. antonyms
8. autobiographical
9. italics
10. false
11. true
12. false
13. false
14. false
15. true
16. true

17. a. Ave.
    b. M.D.
    c. Rev.
18. a. Lisa Lang became homecoming queen.
    b. The Bible says God created heaven and earth.
19. a. criss-crossed
    b. sixty-three hundred
    c. two-thirds
20. a. son-in-law's
    b. Tim and Ed's
21. a. fathers'-in-law
    b. heroes'
22. a. Jimmy Carter is (1.) President, (2.) a husband, and (3.) a father.
    b. In 1941 (I was only two years old) Pearl Harbor was bombed.
23. a. she's
    b. we're
    c. weren't
    d. isn't
24. accept
25. effects
26. compliment

1.   e
2.   j
3.   a
4.   g
5.   i
6   k
7.   d
8.   b
9.   h
10. f
11. a
12. b
13. d
14. c
15. a
16. a
17. a
18. b
19. b
20. d
21. restrictive
22. subordinate
23. correlative conjunctions
24. an epic
25. inflected
26. adverb clause
27. subordinate conjunctions
28. conjunctive adverbs
29. narrative
30. autobiography
31. theme
32. Any other; any three:
     a. setting or location
     b. time or historical events
     c. author's personal life and attitudes
     or significant moments or turning points, theme

1. d
2. a
3. e
4. b
5. i
6. c
7. f
8. j
9. h
10. g
11. Either order:
    a. clear
    b. concise
12. clincher or concluding
13. Example:
    make the story seem more real
14. five senses
15. expository
16. false
17. true
18. false
19. true
20. true
21. false
22. true
23. false
24. false
25. true
26. b
27. a
28. d
29. d
30. d
31. c
32. a
33. c
34. c
35. d

36. a. F
    b. Example:
    Wherever his friends
    gather, he can be found.
37. a. F
    b. Example:
    Although I needed every
    eraser I could get, I
    managed to finish my
    project.
38. a. F
    b. Example:
    There is nothing worse
    than waking up in the
    middle of the night and
    finding the lights out.
39. a. RO
    b. Example:
    Knowledge of the Bible is
    essential for the Christian
    life, and every Christian
    should read his Bible
    daily.
40. a. RO
    b. Example:
    I really enjoyed the play
    after school today, and I
    didn't even miss leaving
    at 3:30.
41. a. F
    b. Example:
    Aged and lonely after
    long years that she
    spent in the prison
    camp, she was finally
    released by the Allies.

1. false
2. true
3. false
4. true
5. false
6. true
7. false
8. true
9. true
10. false
11. d
12. k
13. f
14. g
15. c
16. e
17. h
18. a
19. i
20. j
21. Any order:
    a. friendly letter
    b. invitation
    c. thank-you
22. Any order:
    a. application
    b. order letter
    c. adjustment letter
23. primary
24. Any order:
    a. metaphor
    b. simile
    c. exaggeration
    d. irony
25. Example:
    gather news and furnish it to
    many different papers
26. inside address

27. News magazines are more specialized in content and are directed to special interest groups and the general public. They contain special events and world affairs rather than daily local events of less importance.

28. Example:
    He should be a sympathetic, concerned listener. He should understand the process of listening, the interpretation of literal and implied meanings, the interpretation of figures of speech, and the evaluation of both tone and nonverbal meaning or body language.

1. e
2. h
3. g
4. a
5. k
6. j
7. c
8. f
9. i
10. b
11. false
12. true
13. false
14. false
15. true
16. true
17. true
18. false
19. true
20. true
21. process and analysis
22. near the word it modifies
23. Old Norse, Latin, or Sanskrit
24. Geoffrey Chaucer
25. Any order:
    a. indicative
    b. subjunctive
    c. imperative
26. pentad
27. etymology
28. Either order
    a. borrowing (from another language)
    b. making up (coining) new words
29. Any order:
    a. a thesis
    b. a main body
    c. a conclusion

1. e
2. g
3. i
4. a
5. k
6. h
7. b
8. j
9. f
10. c
11. morpheme
12. brainstorming
13. lead
14. context clues
15. a. concrete
    b. abstract
16. Any order:
    a. subjects
    b. objects
    c. possessives
17. Either order:
    a. intensive
    b. reflexive
18. Any order:
    a. correct spelling
    b. correct meaning
    c. correct (proper) usage
    or part of speech, pronunciation,
    syllable division, etymology
19. Either order:
    a. inform
    b. entertain
20. facts
21. true
22. false
23. false
24. false
25. true
26. true
27. false
28. true
29. true
30. false
31. Example: Speeches are given to inform, to persuade, or to entertain an audience.
32. Example: Sequence is the order in which items, events, or ideas are arranged. Sequence can be chronological, spatial, general to particular, or particular to general.
33. Example: It is a nonfiction (true) account of the author's life or experiences. It contains setting, time, facts about the author's personal life, turning points in his life, and the theme.